THE EXPERTS AGREE:
Strategic Job Jumping
Will Get You Where You Want to Be!

"Well-planned job jumping between companies can turbo-charge your progress. This book shows you how."

—*Giles Goodhead, publisher,*
The Directory of Executive Recruiters
Kennedy Information, LLC

"In today's world of downsizing and restructuring, this is an excellent guide for how to balance career and life planning."

—*E. Kirby Warren, professor of management
and director of The Management Institute,
Columbia University Graduate School of Business*

"This is a great book for learning how to double- and triple-jump your career and leap ahead of the competition."

—*Dr. Robert Kriegel, author of*
If It Ain't Broke . . . BREAK IT!

"This book provides a great headshift. It shows how to maximize your career opportunities by levering your knowledge and skills in several, not just one, company."

—*Jeff Rushton, president,
Transitions Support Management, Inc.*

"A great source for work situations that may confront all of us. It's required reading for my key employees."

—*Lyle Schulman, executive vice president,
Hartford Financial Services, Inc.*

STRATEGIC
JOB JUMPING

Fifty Very Smart Tactics
for Building Your Career

Julia Hartman

PRIMA PUBLISHING

A great deal of care has been taken to provide accurate and current information, however, the ideas, suggestions, general principles, and conclusions presented in this book are those of the author. Readers are urged to consult legal counsel regarding any points of law, their tax advisor regarding tax issues, and their other advisors as appropriate. This publication is not intended as a substitute for competent legal, tax, or other professional advice.

Investment decisions have certain inherent risks. Prima therefore disclaims any warranties or representations, whether express or implied, concerning the accuracy or completeness of the information or advice contained in this book. Any investment a reader may make based on such information is at the reader's sole risk. You should carefully research or consult a qualified financial advisor before making any particular investment.

PRIMA PUBLISHING and colophon are registered trademarks of Prima Communications, Inc.

Library of Congress Cataloging-in-Publication Data
Hartman, Julia.
 Strategic job jumping : fifty very smart tactics for building your career / Julia Hartman.
  p. cm.
 Includes index.
 ISBN 0-7615-1023-0
 1. Career changes. 2. Career development. 3. Job hunting. I. Title.
 HF5384.H374 1997
 650.14—dc21   97-9005
                   CIP

97 98 99 00 01 HH 10 9 8 7 6 5 4 3 2
Printed in the United States of America

HOW TO ORDER

Single copies may be ordered from Prima Publishing, P.O. Box 1260BK, Rocklin, CA 95677; telephone (916) 632-4400. Quantity discounts are available. On your letterhead, include information concerning the intended use of the books and the number of books you wish to purchase.

VISIT US ONLINE AT HTTP://WWW.PRIMAPUBLISHING.COM

CONTENTS

PART TWO: Jumpers at Home

Part Three: People Jumping to the Top

ACKNOWLEDGMENTS

To all the people who encouraged me to write this book: Thank you. Shelley, my husband, thanks for insisting that I tell all. Rafe Sagalyn and Ethan Kline at the Sagalyn Literary Agency, thank you for choosing my project and finding a publisher. Many thanks go to the entire team at Prima, who all worked together to keep on schedule for an early publication date. Georgia Hughes, acquisitions editor, Prima Publishing, thank you for discovering the manuscript and shaping it to completion.

Richard Simon, thank you for dropping by often with books and ideas. Thank you to the all the people who contributed to the project, specifically the executives and recruiters who told their stories. Lastly, thank you to all of my employers, who were a great source of inspiration.

INTRODUCTION

My first job out of college was as a violinist in an orchestra in Salzburg, Austria, that paid $200 a week. Fourteen years later I accepted a position as vice president, chief marketing officer, within a global corporation, with an annual compensation package of $165,000. During that fourteen-year period, I earned an MBA from Columbia Business School, worked for nine companies in marketing and sales, moved five times (including three corporate relocations), and built a networking database of 1,702 people. As you can see, job jumping is a topic close to my heart.

This book is a modern, plain-talking, "street smart" story about how to enjoy and profit from today's world of downsizing and turbulence. You will learn about my wild ride through a variety of typical corporate perils and pick up job-jumping techniques that work. This book includes lots of juicy employment negotiation dialogues—what they said, what I said. Check out Chapter Seven, "Get Paid Coming and Going," for an example. Ask for that signing or exit bonus by using the bonus dialogues in that chapter to create your own winning strategy. Negotiate the rest of your compensation by using the compensation dialogues in Chapter Eight as guides. Find out three common interview objections to job jumping in Chapter Five and learn responses that worked. There are even seasonal benefits to job jumping; find out when it's the season to be paid.

Have you ventured into the "dark side" of employment and wondered about legal issues? Have you ever thought about creating an employment contract that would protect you in court? If so, read Chapter Nine, "A Painless Overview of Employment Contracts and Employment Law," which features an interview with a renowned employment lawyer. Learn who's getting employment contracts and what they include. If you've been laid-off or fired (and treated with the "utmost dignity and respect"), learn how to find out what your past employers are saying about you.

Discover how to build your career and financial future by looking out for yourself and gain the confidence that looking out for yourself is the very best thing you can do for any employer. Frankly, in today's environment, sometimes the best thing you can do—for your own career and for your employer—is to change jobs, either within your current company or by moving to another company.

If you earn a promotion within your current firm, you have become a more efficient employee and can improve your firm's productivity. If you decide to change firms within the same industry to gain greater responsibility and salary, you benefit both the firm that you leave and the firm that you join. The firm that you leave has the opportunity, through an exit interview with you, to learn how to improve their employee retention and consequently become more productive and competitive. The firm that you join has the benefit of your broader industry experience. With your help they may learn how to create and dominate the future of that industry.

A study by the American Management Association concluded that fewer than half of the firms that have downsized in the past five years have subsequently increased their profits and that only a third have reported higher productivity. According to studies by Frederick Reichheld, a director of Bain & Company and author of *The Loyalty Effect*, some firms today are losing employees as fast as they are losing customers (Harvard Business School Press, 1996, pp. 4, 95). These firms cannot compete as effectively as firms that learn how to retain employees, customers, and investors. *Today, employees need to find companies worth working for.*

How often should you change jobs? Learn the perspectives offered by recruiters and other human resource professionals in Chapter Six. See how supply and demand shape perceptions of the acceptability of job jumping.

Can you conduct an automated job search? I've done it for years. Learn how to use your own personal database with an easy contact management system in Chapter Four. You don't have to be a techno-nerd to do this.

How many times have you wondered whether you should relocate? The Jumper Credo in Chapter Three describes fourteen ways to get into the mind-set for changing jobs. Should you own or rent your new residence? Learn a systematic way to evaluate this and discover nine personal financial tactics that specifically support changing jobs in Chapter Ten.

Would you like some examples from people on their way up? Chapter Twelve features stories and advice from nine executives who are jumping to the top. One is a CEO of a major corporation, one is an entrepreneur, and the others are executives in the fields of advertising, human resources, sales, technology, temporary staffing, and non-profit.

Gain the confidence to *go for it*. As you study these pages, you will discover modern techniques that will fuel your leaps into the future.

Part One

Jumpers at Work

My First
Big
Jumps

Tactics 1–4:

1. Do what you want
2. Get paid to play
3. The family business incubator
4. A Columbia MBA degree can open doors

found that it took practice to enjoy changing jobs. My first job change was the most difficult; the next were easier. Then I grew to expect and enjoy the process of change itself. My first job? I was a musician.

Do What You Want

I started playing the violin at age thirteen. It was wonderful and I knew it had to be part of my future. I loved playing and was convinced that it was worth my time. So I played second violin in the public school orchestra through high school. Although starting the violin at age thirteen is too late to be great, I did not care about being great. I wanted to play, however I could. When I told my parents that I wanted to go to music school they tried to dissuade me. They warned me that they would not support me after I got my bachelor's degree. Some schools that I applied to asked if I wanted to learn how to be a music teacher; no, I wanted the violin performance curriculum.

I was finally accepted at Boston University School for the Arts. One day I went to a concert and heard the assistant concertmaster of the Boston Symphony. He made the sound that I wanted to make. I played for him and asked if he would please teach me. He finally agreed but told me that I would need to start over. I did. It took me six years to get to the level where he would allow me to play my senior recital. During that time I played in the last few rows of the second violin section in the school's "B" orchestra.

Get Paid to Play

I had the time of my life in music school! I played in recording studios, played in the Vermont Symphony, played electric violin in a band, and I was convinced that playing music was going to be my profession. But it was obvious by my junior year at college that I would not be able to support myself playing in community orchestras in the United States. I went to the music school library and researched. Where in the world could I get paid to play the violin? I discovered that there were plenty of opportunities in Germany, Austria, Italy, and

South America. I made a tape, got it copied, and sent it all over the world.

One day I found a German contract in the mail. I took it over to a neighbor who spoke German; it was an offer to play in a summer orchestra in Salzburg, Austria, which paid enough to support me but did not include the cost of the plane ticket. My parents would not lend me the money but offered to co-sign a bank loan. I got the loan, packed a huge trunk, and planned to leave the United States for about five years. The orchestra was wonderful! We played in magnificent concert halls; halls that Mozart had played in. The orchestra was composed of people from all over the world; our only common language was music. We lived in dorms together and learned to communicate.

My orchestra colleagues showed me how to get a permanent job playing in a German or Austrian orchestra. They helped me write my *lebenslauf,* a handwritten musical resume. They introduced me to the musical trade magazine, *Das Orchestra,* where I could find orchestral employment ads. My U.S. violin teacher found me a teacher in Austria; he found it ironic that his least advanced student had a paying music job for the summer. My Austrian teacher taught me the orchestral excerpts I was required to know in Europe.

In November, at age twenty-four, eleven years after my musical quest began, I won an audition. I received a life-long contract as an orchestral violinist in a remote Austrian village. It paid enough to live on. I could buy a car. I could sign an apartment lease. I could buy clothes and eat. But I felt like I was a third gender. The remainder of the orchestra was 100 percent male, generally in their forties and up. They went home to wives who wore long traditional dresses, with push-up bras. I felt a bit out of place wearing pants and speaking English. The only German words I knew were musical terms like "slower" and "faster" . . . and the lack of 24-hour convenience stores was appalling.

The Family Business Incubator

But it was more than that. I couldn't find a band to play electric violin with and I was getting sick of playing the classics. For the first time in my life, men with money seemed to have a strange allure. So I went back to the United States and decided to switch careers. I tried to get into a bank training program in my hometown but I might as well have been from Mars, fresh from Austria with my bachelor of music degree. My parents, however, had the best job going—they were running a fast-growing group-travel tour company—and they offered me a job where I could travel and do sales presentations to groups. I accepted their offer. Their job was really fun and I learned a lot about marketing and sales.

A Columbia MBA Degree Can Open Doors

Meanwhile, my brother was accepted at the Wharton School of Business. I figured that if my brother could get into Wharton, well, then I could get in anywhere! After three years in the family business, I applied to Columbia Business School and was accepted. Three weeks after starting school, we had the opportunity to sign up for summer internship interviews. We had our choice of all the big banks and I was thrilled.

This was my first experience with the power of credentials in business. After just three weeks in a "top ten" business school, I could land interviews with the largest banks in the United States. Three years earlier, with my Bachelor of Music degree, I couldn't get interviews with my hometown banks. Did I morph in three years and three weeks? No. It was the power of the business school credentials.

I chose Citibank for my summer internship and for my first job after completing my MBA. Aside from the blue-chip Citibank name, the people at Citibank were truly passionate. They were pioneering direct marketing, wanted to be the best, and wanted people to help them figure out this new marketing strategy. In addition, they had some powerful women leaders at Citibank. If they could get there, I thought I could too! The packaged-goods firms, on the other hand, wanted to teach people how to do mass marketing—their way. Given the fantastic marketing education that Columbia provided, it was easy to see the trends and the rise of direct marketing. I wanted to do direct marketing and Citibank wanted to pay.

It was great to work at Citibank. We had many resources. We had clear and passionate leadership imploring us to "figure it out." We did our best and I loved my new career. But after a while I noticed that I could be paid more outside of Citibank. I also noticed that I could be paid to leave Citibank.

My curiosity grew about the entire direct-marketing industry. Then I wondered how to best use my direct-marketing skills . . . should I be a consultant, an employee, or a contracted employee? What was the best way to structure my career? What would be the future trends in employment? How could my career moves capitalize on these trends?

At this point, I began developing the job-jumping tactics that have since fueled my career and ensured that I've never felt forced to stay at a job. These job-jumping strategies have helped me in times of corporate downsizing and restructuring—topics of the next chapter, which explores the key trends fueling job change.

2

Growth of the Jumper Movement

Topics:
- Outsourcing: Its future and your role
- Downsizing and the growth of small firms
- The growth of contract employment
- Key-employee retention programs

f you are thinking about changing jobs, you may be wondering how much of your decision is personal and how much may just reflect current trends in employment. Are you the primary driver directing your job changes or are trends in employment directing your job changes?

This chapter explores trends in employment and shows how they are likely to affect your current and future jobs. I examine historical data on outsourcing, downsizing, the growth of small firms, contract employment, and key employee-retention programs. For some of us, changing jobs is the strongest career strategy. This research is intended to put your job-change questions within the larger context of the employment trends in our society. Arm yourself with knowledge. Gain confidence. If you decide that a job change is for you, *go for it!*

Outsourcing: Its Future and Your Role

Today, companies do not make everything that they sell; instead they contract with outside suppliers, a practice known as *outsourcing*. Outsourcing is emerging as a competitive weapon for corporations across many different industries. This fast-growing trend can build revenue as well as cut costs.

The managing partner of Price Waterhouse's consulting group predicts that we're at the beginning of an explosion in outsourcing ("Has Outsourcing Gone Too Far?" *Business Week,* 4/1/96). According to a poll by consultant A. T. Kearney, which surveyed twenty-six major companies, including American Airlines, DuPont, Exxon, Honda, IBM, and Johnson & Johnson, about 86 percent of major corporations now outsource at least some services, up from 58 percent in 1992 (*Business Week,* 4/1/96).

However, don't expect to see outsourcing just in the automotive or staffing industries. According to data released from the Outsourcing Institute, of the $100 billion spent annually on outsourcing, 40 percent is in information technology; 30 percent is in distribution, property, plant management, and other blue collar areas; and 30 percent is in administration, personnel, customer service, finance, sales, and other white-collar activities ("Comment & Analysis: In, Out, Shake It All About," *Financial Times,* 5/16/96). Marketing, sales, customer service, and engineering functions are being outsourced, and this trend has spread to countless industries, including technology, aviation, and health care.

Why are companies outsourcing? In one industry survey, 50 percent outsourced "when others can do it better, 35 percent outsourced to focus on their core business, and 32 percent outsourced to reduce their cost base" ("Rumble of Discontent from Clients," *Financial Times*, 5/1/96).

Are you hearing the term *core business* a lot lately? The above study, which surveyed over 1,000 directors and senior managers, found that there were only *three* activities that more than 35 percent of the companies regarded as "core": business strategy, information technology strategy, and new product development. Two-thirds of those surveyed regarded everything else as non-core—including research and development, customer handling, and finance and accounting.

What can we expect from this trend toward outsourcing? Expect to see it expand and go global. Companies will shift from outsourcing on a country-by-country basis to choosing global strategic outsourcing partners (*Financial Times*, 5/1/96).

How does this affect your job and job prospects? First of all, you need to personally come to terms with this trend because it's highly likely to affect your career. It's a big magilla and it's charging right at you. Knowledge about outsourcing is valuable and in demand. If you can learn how to outsource a function, or if you can work for an outsourcing company, you will have the knowledge that is needed today and in the future. Consequently, experience in outsourcing will increase your prospects for getting jobs.

In some cases, as a manager, you could lose your job if you decide *not* to outsource. What would happen if outsourcing could raise revenue, or cut costs, or both? What if you, the manager, do not take the leap to do it? The company may decide to hire someone else to manage your project. What could happen to the competitiveness of your firm if your firm does not outsource and your competitors are benefiting by outsourcing? Realize that outsourcing is another opportunity for you personally to gain responsibility.

Downsizing and the Growth of Small Firms

When will downsizing end? According to the British consultant Charles Handy, who has been writing books on the American workplace for decades, "'Never'" ("How Safe Is Your Job?" *Fortune Magazine*, 4/1/96). A recent survey by the American Management Association estimated that 60 percent of the companies surveyed would eliminate jobs over the next year, which was the highest percentage in the survey's history (*Fortune*, 4/1/96).

But demand for managers is huge and, based on U.S. Bureau of Labor statistics, growing faster than the overall employment rate. "Managerial employment, which includes managers, executives, and administrators, totaled 17.7 million workers for the second quarter of 1996, a 4.7% increase from the year-earlier period, according to U.S. Bureau of Labor Statistics. That compares with only a 1.3% increase in overall employment over the same period" ("Firms' Demands for Managers Is Growing," *Wall Street Journal*, 9/26/96).

The Bureau of Labor Statistics also reports that unemployment among managers has fallen 20 percent since 1993. "'When you move from cost-cutting to growth strategies, you've got to add management talent,' says Paul Ray, Jr., Chairman of the Association of Executive Search Consultants" (*Wall Street Journal*, 9/26/96).

Trend data also clearly show that employment in small firms is increasing faster than employment in large firms. According to an analysis of Census Bureau data, "Between 1980 and 1992, there was a 28.1 percent increase in jobs in small businesses, to 11.4 million. Businesses with more than 100 employees created 6.6 million new jobs in the same period, a 19.3 percent increase" ("Small Businesses Make a Big Dent in Unemployment Rolls," *Chicago Tribune*, 4/21/96). Although total employment in Fortune 500 companies has steadily decreased since 1979, the number of business establishments employing between 50 and 500 workers has grown 36 percent over the same period (*Wall Street Journal*, 9/26/96).

What can we expect from these trends? According to Charles Handy, expect to see big companies directly employing a small group of core managers. "Every successful organization will tell you that they have at least quadrupled their turnover in the last ten years but have halved their professional core" (*The Age of Unreason*, Harvard Business School Press, 1989, p. 91). The managerial group is responsible for outsourcing many of the functions that were formerly internal.

What do you do about this trend? Use a defensive tactical strategy—build marketable skills that you enjoy, ones that could eventually support you in a small firm or enable you to open your own firm. Developing marketable skills means that you have to get those assignments that enable you to *learn* marketable skills. You are competing with others to get these projects and your future depends on which projects you win. This defensive strategy may even work if you are determined to be one of the few running big firms in the future. If you plan on running a big firm, however, you also need to bet right on which companies are going to be big down the road.

The Growth of Contract Employment

Temporary help first became popular with clerical workers and within less-skilled professions. Now, however, managers also can be temporary, *interim,* or *contracted* for a particular time period. According to the National Association of Temporary and Staffing Services, in 1995 there were 2.16 million temporaries in the U.S. workforce, up 10 percent from the previous year, and close to double that of five years ago ("Trading Briefcases for Little League Games," *PR Newswire,* 5/30/96). In 1994 temporary workers comprised 1.65 percent of the total U.S. workforce. Approximately 4.8 percent of temporary workers were categorized as professionals and an additional 11.2 percent as technical.

According to Kennedy Publications' *The Directory of Executive Temporary Placement Firms* (1995), there were 229 temporary placement firms for executives in 1995, which is an increase of 420 percent over the 44 firms identified in 1990. The major players are IMCOR and Management Recruiters International. These firms receive a fee of 20 to 35 percent of compensation (this fee is paid by the client firm, not you).

Companies hire interim executives for a number of reasons. Sometimes an interim worker will fill in or try out for a position during a search for a long-term employee. Other times, contracted employees are hired to complete a specific, short-term project. After companies have downsized, they may not have the management talent left to run specific functions (such as human resources, marketing, or accounting), and interim executives are then hired on an as-needed basis. The use of contract employees provides flexibility to firms.

How could this affect your job? If you are performing a specialized non-core function, there is the possibility that your job will be outsourced in the future. This possibility could provide you with more flexibility in lifestyle and could affect your compensation—upward or downward. As an interim or contracted employee, you generally need to contract your benefits individually, but this is also possible (see Chapter Ten).

A contracted position may also be a good way for you to try out for a new longer-term position and could be of benefit while conducting a job search. As insurance for the future, it is a good idea to find out which executive temporary placement firms specialize in your function or industry even if you're happily employed.

Key-Employee Retention Programs

Amid the downsizing and turmoil there are signs that smart companies are beginning to learn the value of key employees. These companies are succeeding because they are building their franchises by retaining customers, employees, and investors. Employee retention programs include incentive compensation and analysis of employee attrition. As Peter Drucker says:

> All organizations now say routinely, "People are our greatest asset." Yet few practice what they preach, let alone truly believe it. Most still believe, though

perhaps not consciously, what nineteenth-century employers believed: people need us more than we need them. But, in fact, organizations have to market membership as much as they market products and services—and perhaps more. They have to attract people, hold people, recognize and reward people, motivate people, and serve and satisfy people. (Frederick Reichheld quoting Drucker in *The Loyalty Effect*, Harvard Business School Press, 1996)

It's common knowledge that it costs far less to retain a current customer than to acquire a new one. According to Don Peppers and Martha Rogers, "If your company is typical, it costs you five times as much to get a single new customer as it does to keep one you already have" (*The One to One Future*, Doubleday, 1993). This makes intuitive sense; a bucket is difficult to fill if it's constantly leaking.

In *The Loyalty Effect*, Frederick Reichheld expands the leaky-bucket theory to include employees and investors. Reichheld documents that companies are more successful than their competitors when they are able to retain employees, customers, and investors. He calls these companies "loyalty leaders." "By sharing the spoils of loyalty with their employees, [loyalty leaders] have built a tenure-based productivity advantage. In many cases, their average employee duration is 50 to 100 percent better than the competition's. In such companies, learning persists and grows. In companies where employees perpetually leave in mid-career, learning is forever falling back to nil" (p. 128).

Reichheld makes the point that companies need to increase their productivity by aligning employee compensation with employee productivity. Unfortunately, many businesses fail to share their profits, and thus fail to develop their employees' full productivity potential. A company that doesn't develop this enormous productivity potential loses when it competes against a company that does develop its employees' potential. The employees working for the losing company lose twice—first losing the opportunity to develop to their full potential and second losing financially because they are not working for the higher-paying, winning company.

According to Reichheld, a corollary to his theory also holds true:

> There is growing evidence that over the long term, firms that resort to frequent or massive layoffs significantly underperform the market. The *Economist* reported recently on a study by the American Management Association which concluded that fewer than half of the firms that have downsized in the past five years have subsequently increased their profits, and that only a third have reported higher productivity. Another study, reported in the *Wall Street Journal,* found that downsizing companies outperform the S&P only slightly during the six months following news of a restructuring, then lag badly, netting a negative 24 percent by the end of three years. This really should come as no surprise. Companies forced to jettison their human assets should be worth less. (p. 95)

How do the trends in key-employee compensation programs affect your job and job prospects? Look for companies that encourage employees to create value by sharing that value with their employees. Reichheld says, "The key is to compensate partner-employees by sharing the value they help to create for customers" (p. 23). This can take the form of incentive compensation. According to surveys by Hewitt Associates, approximately

61 percent of large and medium-size companies now offer profit-sharing, bonus awards, and other kinds of variable pay, up from 47 percent in 1990 ("Don't Count on That Merit Raise This Year," *Wall Street Journal*, 1/7/97).

Another litmus test to use when you are searching for companies that value employees is to find out whether they categorize the quantity and type of employee attrition. Reichheld says, "The best firms don't simply track defection rates; they categorize departures and then track defection rates by category" (p. 99). In these companies, top management tries to avoid growth in categories of employees who leave for competitors, or because they don't like their jobs. When this type of defection occurs, they analyze the reasons in order to help create changes in the company.

One way to investigate this is after receiving an offer of employment is to ask if the firm keeps statistics on employee attrition and if they will share them with you. If the firm doesn't have any idea how many employees have left, or why, they do not show signs of truly valuing their employees. One firm I visited had a super retention rate. When I asked them how they accomplished this, they said that they thought of their employees as assets rather than liabilities. Because the employees figured out what new products to sell, and ran the business, the managers regarded employee ideas as assets, ones which needed to be cultivated.

Summary

Today, companies are immersed in a quickly changing environment. Outsourcing and downsizing affect the stability of your job and need to be assessed in each of your career moves. Contract employment and key-employee retention programs may present new opportunities.

How do you capitalize on these trends? Learn the benefits of job-jumping for both employers and employees in Chapter Three.

CHAPTER

3

Jumpers Transform the Future

L et's start with a technical definition of jumpers and what makes them special, review the benefits of this type of career to both jumpers and their employers, and then explore jumpers' career-building strategies.

What Is a Jumper?

Jumpers are people capitalizing on the employment trends we examined in the last chapter. They are not being hurt by downsizing; they are not lamenting the lack of stability in today's job world. Just the opposite, in fact: Jumpers are profiting from these market conditions. Jumpers are leaders; they are front-runners. Jumpers are not the only ones profiting from their career strategy—the firms they join benefit by hiring them.

Jumpers are people who have built successful careers in business, generally within one industry or profession, by completing a series of jobs with different companies. These assignments can be contracted for a certain time period, can be a series of traditional jobs, or can be a combination of these two employment structures. There are several different types of jumpers. Some stay at their first job for several years and then move to a series of firms in shorter-term assignments. Some jumpers change firms every three to four years and stay at this pace throughout their careers. It is also common for jumpers to make a series of jumps and then stay at their optimum assignment.

As a result of gaining experience from many assignments within the same industry, jumpers have a broad industry perspective, which may further the strategic vision of their employers. For example, in the direct-marketing industry, there are mailing list vendors, firms that conduct direct-marketing campaigns, firms that provide research for conducting direct-marketing campaigns, firms that sell direct-mail advertising space, telemarketing firms, and many others. Jumpers in the direct-marketing field have a well-rounded industry perspective because they have worked in many different firms within the same industry. Being familiar with many different jobs within their industry, jumpers have become specialists in their particular industry.

This logic holds true with jumpers who've used another career-building strategy, those who have built successful careers within a particular profession in many *different* industries. For example, someone in a government relations career may start out in the government and then move to a series of assignments with different firms, in diverse industries, while still remaining a specialist in government relations.

Five Benefits Jumpers Bring to Employers

How does the broader industry vision of the jumper benefit their employers? Let's refer to some acknowledged experts in management consulting: Gary Hamel and C. K. Prahalad. According to *Business Week,* their book, *Competing for the Future* (Harvard Business School Press, 1994), encourages firms to build their strategic plans by transforming the future of their industries:

> Our goal in this book is to enlarge the concept of strategy so that it more fully encompasses the emerging competitive reality—a reality in which the goal is to transform industries, not just organizations; a reality in which being incrementally better is not enough; a reality in which any company that cannot imagine the future won't be around to enjoy it [p. xviii]. . . . In business, as in art, what distinguishes leaders from laggards, and greatness from mediocrity, is the ability to uniquely imagine what could be. (p. 27)

The industry perspective developed by jumpers not only forwards the strategic vision of their employers, it can also help those employers transform the industry. Jumpers who have worked for competing firms in the same industry may be the most qualified people to analyze the future of that industry.

Jumpers earned this industry perspective by taking on a great deal of personal risk in order to accept new assignments. Consequently jumpers have more than just an industry vision; they have broad firsthand industry experience and confidence in their industry vision!

"Harassment of the corporation" is another benefit that jumpers bring to their employers. Harassment takes on a new meaning here. Jumpers (harassers) are the catalysts, not the victims, and corporations are the beneficiaries! Jumpers "hassle" their employers to be better, more competitive performers in strategic planning, in new product development, and in operations. They see things that longer-term, "loyal" employees just don't. Jumpers are not susceptible to "group think" or "the way it has always been done." Jumpers have confidence in their convictions and ample opportunity to walk if frustrated.

The concept of "harassment of the corporation" is very similar to the concept of competition. Competition helps companies to grow and change. Because jumpers bring an industry perspective, they can bring the views of competitors to their current employers. Although it may not be enjoyable for a company to learn about its weaknesses, it improves a company to become aware of them. It may take a jumper's harassment to lead a company to change for the better.

Jumpers bring their employers the following benefits:

1. A broader industry prospective, which can increase the company's strategic vision,

2. A short-term perspective in which to make a difference in the organization,

3. Numerous contacts, which can benefit the organization,

4. Above-average education and training,

5. An impetus to change in order to embrace winning strategies.

Jumpers thrive on change. They want to transform their companies faster than the "loyal" employees do. In fact, "loyal" employees may not have the skills to change business as usual. They may lack the industry perspective of jumpers and confidence in their convictions. They may not see the future as clearly as jumpers do.

Let's look at this practically: "loyal" employees probably don't know how to jump. They have stayed in the same position year after year. Sometimes "loyal" employees personally can't afford to make risky decisions. Would someone else hire them if they failed? *If someone hasn't managed change personally, they're unlikely to be capable of doing it for an employer.* If "loyal" employees are in leadership positions, many will take the no-risk (and no-reward) business strategy, trying to protect their jobs.

Jumping Is a Savvy Career-Management Strategy

Jumping is a win–win strategy with benefits to employees and employers. Many of the benefits that jumpers bring to their employers also benefit themselves.

Your Broader Industry Perspective Furthers Your Strategic Vision

When you work for several different companies in one industry, you will gain a broader perspective on that industry than if you worked for just one company in the industry. Given your broader perspective, you are in a position to provide valuable input to the strategic direction of your company. A key ingredient in your strategic vision will be your ability to recognize functions that companies duplicate and areas where companies are entirely different. Because jumpers have firsthand experience with the strengths and weaknesses of vendors and competitors in their industry, they tend to have a lot of knowledge that can be used in new product development and strategic planning. People who have worked for only one or two companies will not have this broader base and thus will not see the opportunities that jumpers see.

For example, in Section Three, you will read about John, a salesperson who worked for the top two companies in one industry. He jumped to a sales job with a third competitor in that industry. Six months after working at the third company, he was promoted to director of new product development. The company felt that John, who had worked for the top competitors in the industry, had the best experience to lead their new product development strategy.

Your Numerous Contacts Benefit You Professionally

Because savvy jumpers keep a database of their contacts, they have a reference for whom to call when their firm does not have a needed resource. Your contact database can become a competitive weapon for you personally as well as a benefit to your company. You may know the top prospects for a product, the top candidates for a job, the best company for outsourcing, and so on. You can easily query your database and provide great contacts, instantly. I use my personal database every day to help my employers, my friends, and myself.

You Have a Shorter Time Frame
in Which to Make a Difference

As a jumper, you think, "I need to finish this assignment because I need this accomplishment before going on to the next assignment." You are new to the job and want to get it done quickly. You pack your time with critical assignments that provide the experience you need to advance.

Your Confidence and Conviction Grow with Every Jump

Learning to jump means learning to assimilate change at a faster pace. As you learn to roll with the punches, you become more confident in your own judgment. This enables you to speak more clearly at meetings and presentations and helps you to grow professionally. Dealing with constant change, you also become acquainted with your weaknesses and confront them more often. It's not easy to adjust to new job after new job, but that's what makes it fun. If it *was* easy, they wouldn't need a jumper!

The Numerous Financial Benefits of Jumping

In many positions, there is little opportunity to increase your salary by a magnitude. Obviously, with jumping, the sky's the limit. You can substantially increase your salary, bonuses, and other compensation by jumping. (See Chapters Seven and Eight for more information on how to do this.)

The Personal Benefits of Jumping

My family and I have enjoyed living in many diverse communities. We've lived in major cities and suburbs and in many different types of residences. Each was an adventure and each was fun. We enjoyed meeting new people and enjoyed the house hunting. Each new environment has enabled each person in my family to learn about his or her preferences. We may choose to settle down some day. By the time we do that, we will know exactly what type of community and residence we prefer.

Why Do Jumpers Jump?

I've been interviewing jumpers for several years and it has become quite clear to me that jumpers are strong individuals with unique ideas. I've tried to figure out if there are similar traits that could describe the jumpers I know. By analyzing jumpers' careers, I've observed fourteen common practices that support their success. I call these success-building strategies "The Jumper Credo." The strategies begin with what jumpers think about, continue to how they recruit and how they feel about salary negotiations, and finally progress to how they feel about work. The Jumper Credo is not meant to describe every jumper; each is an individual. However, if you analyze jumpers as a group, you will see that these strategies are common to many.

A Closer Look at the Jumper Credo

You Are What You Think, You Become What You Do

All actions begin with a thought. Thus, if you want certain actions as outcomes, you must learn to think appropriately. There are only so many seconds in a day. If you do not think about what you need to think about, you will not be able to produce the desired actions. For example, you are determined to

The Jumper Credo

*Fourteen Strategies for Successful Business Careers
Through Changing Jobs*

1. You are what you think, you become what you do.
2. You need to dream to survive; think about what you want to think about.
3. Try to imagine how great you could become; realize that the sky's the limit.
4. Strive to increase your peripheral vision.
5. What you do is more important than what you have.
6. As in chess, move your piece to the square where it has the most opportunities to influence other pieces.
7. Recruiting is in everything you do.
8. Invest in the people you meet.
9. Your family comes before your job.
10. The most important thing that you bring to your job is your intellectual capital; learn how to grow it.
11. If you're not playing, you're not working.
12. Market pricing should dominate salary negotiations.
13. Get paid on merit whenever possible—on the way in, on the way out, annually, quarterly, and so on.
14. Get paid to play.

be successful in your business career. You do not have time to think about being unsuccessful because every negative thought takes away from time you could be thinking about positive outcomes.

You Need to Dream to Survive;
Think About What You Want to Think About

Just as the mind at night needs to dream, the mind during the day needs to wander. How can you ever discover what you want to do unless you can think about whatever you want? Pretend you are looking at a terrific view from the top of a mountain . . . let your mind wander across all the positive, successful futures you can imagine. It also helps to think about your job with the same expansive mind-set. Now that you've dreamed a little, what strategies do you think your firm should pursue?

Try to Imagine Exactly How Great You Could Become;
Realize That the Sky's the Limit

As you gaze out at the challenges confronting you, visualize that your success will be beyond what you can dream of today. All your actions will lead to future actions, and as they keep going in positive directions there are infinite possibilities for success. How could you possibly be able to imagine them all now?

Strive to Increase Your Peripheral Vision

With every interaction, ask what are the parts that you are *not* seeing? What was *not* said in the book, the conversation, or the article? Your broader vision can lead you to more perceptive thoughts. Consequently, you will be more informed and able to make better decisions.

What You Do Is More Important Than What You Have

Sometimes mind-expanding thoughts conflict . . . If I did such and such, I could have that, but if I did so and so, I could have. . . . Think about what you want to be doing more than what you want to have. If you do what is right for you, what you have will be right for you.

As in Chess, Move Your Piece to the Square Where It Has the Most Opportunities to Influence Other Pieces

If I do action x, I could do actions a, b, and c. But if I do action y, I could do actions d to w. Which actions best influence the possibilities for other actions?

Recruiting Is in Everything You Do

Every moment that you live is an investment in the next moment. Each moment should open up more possibilities for the next. Recognize that recruiting occurs whenever you communicate. It is occurring with whomever you speak, wherever you speak, whatever you do. You are building your success with every single one of your actions.

Invest in the People You Meet

Who will help you to change your life? Generally the people that you know. So pay attention to everyone you meet and be sure that you meet those whom you need to meet. You and the people you know hold the key to your future.

Your Family Comes Before Your Job

Wherever your thoughts may roam or wherever your actions may take you, make sure that your family is comfortable with what is happening. Your family is part of you. Your success needs to feel like a success to your family too.

The Most Important Thing That You Bring to Your Job Is Your Intellectual Capital: Learn How to Grow It

Your unique ideas are critical to your success. When you're on the job, ask yourself these questions: "Am I thinking about what I want to be thinking about? Am I increasing my peripheral vision? Can we wonder together as a group?" When considering a new job, ask yourself what new ideas and perspectives you could bring to that firm. Your ideas distinguish you from other executives; be sure to grow them.

If You're Not Playing, You're Not Working

Are your best ideas accepted by your firm? Are you free to think about what you want to think about? Is it fun at work? Is it thrilling? Are you excited to start work when you wake up in the morning? If the answer isn't "yes" to these questions, then neither you nor your employer are using your time together as effectively as you could be. You cannot afford to waste a moment in your quest to fulfill your dreams. Dreamers are leaders.

Market Pricing Should Dominate Salary Negotiations

Life is short; you have an extremely limited amount of time to pursue each of your best strategies to success. You may have a series of potential jumps mapped out or you may need to make a particular jump to open up broader horizons. If the entire compensation package is not the most competitive for your skills, then ask yourself why.

It's common for large employers with bureaucratic human resource policies to lag on salary increases for their employees.

They don't structure compensation that shares the value you create for the firm. If you could earn a jump up elsewhere, your employer does not fully value the attractiveness of your skills. Is this a smart way for your employer to do business? Do you want to work for an employer that doesn't understand your value to the firm? Will this firm win in the industry if it doesn't retain its employees? Will you advance to your successful future if you don't get through this roadblock?

If you are considering a new employer that does not offer market price, increase your recruiting efforts to get competing offers. Once you have at least one competing offer, the value of your skills will be clearer to everyone concerned.

Get Paid on Merit Whenever Possible— On the Way in, On the Way out, Annually, Quarterly, and So On

Stand up for your right to be paid for your work. Look to share the value you create for the firm. Every company compensates differently and for different reasons. The current environment supports unequal and unpredictable payments for exit, signing, and other bonuses. Know the parameters. If you can find the opportunity to be paid on merit, go for it!

Get Paid to Play

Now that you've decided what to think about and what to do, you should get paid doing it. Enjoy it. Dream about it during the day and at night. Be passionate! Give it all you've got.

Summary

Consider all the benefits of being a jumper and the benefits that jumpers bring to their employers. Jumpers have broader strategic vision, make a difference in the short term, are highly educated, and impel their companies to embrace winning strategies.

Jumpers transform the future. They have the industry experience and education to allow their intellect to reign. They are not bound by the mores of any company. They have confidence in their views and they can afford to express them.

Now that you know the advantages of being a jumper, and their strategies for success, you'll want to perfect your jumping skills. Read on to learn

■ how to promote yourself,

■ how to keep finding the best job for yourself,

■ how to defend your jumps in job interviews,

■ how to get paid coming and going,

■ how to negotiate your compensation package,

■ and how to lead the lifestyle of a jumper!

Self-Promotion: My Database, My Life

Tactics 5–13:

5. Establish a permanent phone number
6. Create a contact database
7. Package yourself on paper
8. Create a home page and package yourself electronically
9. Package your work and use it to gain control of the interview agenda
10. Gain control of the telephone interview agenda
11. Create opportunities to feed your database
12. Use your database to promote yourself
13. Promote yourself regularly to recruiters

L ife is a numbers game. If you want the very best for yourself, accept that you are only one of the numbers. Accept that everyone else you know is only one of the numbers. With that being said, what are the chances of someone you know telling you about a great career opportunity? If you know five people, your chances are that five people may come to you with this news. If you know 500 people, your chances have just increased 9,900 percent. But how do you get to know 500 people? It's a way of life and I'm going to give you the rules to live by.

Establish a Permanent Phone Number

Put your permanent phone number on your business cards if possible. Self-promotion is a lifelong activity. Each time you interact with someone, you are investing in self-promotion. Every action you take to promote yourself impacts the rest of your life to some degree. Your goal is to keep your professional name and phone number the same for as long as you continue investing in self-promotion. This makes it easy for people to contact you.

If you think that you might move in the next five years, set up a remote voicemail phone number. I use the Message Bank in New York City; dial 212-969-0631 to hear my "virtual office." The message provides my local phone number, my fax number, and the electronic addresses for my Internet home-page and electronic mail. Because I have moved a lot, this permanent phone number has enabled people to keep in touch with me.

If you think that you can afford it long-term, set up a permanent address with a private post office service and/or your own domain name on the Internet. Private post office services will forward your mail. My experience with the U.S. Postal Service is that they will not forward mail long-term from post office boxes (regardless of what they say!).

I've elected to keep a permanent e-mail address forwarded through my website: jh@juliahartman.com. This way I can change e-mail providers and still keep the same address. E-mail fosters conversations just like the phone. I personally haven't found a permanent snail-mail post office box to be cost-effective.

Create a Contact Database

You can buy non-technical database programs at any computer software store. (I use ACT.) Categorize your contacts by how you interact with them. I have over fifty business categories and twenty-five personal categories. Professionally, I consult to the direct-marketing industry; these classifications include printer, telemarketing, mailing list vendor, ad agencies, and industry classifications including financial services, telecommunications, retail, and automotive. Keep your database at work and at home. Whenever you talk to someone, keep a record of his or her name, address, phone, e-mail address, and notes in your database. Keep your computer on and your database running all the time.

Your database program must enable you to do searches of contacts by industry, create instant personalized letters to a group of contacts, and create instant mailing labels. It should include an area for notes to keep track of so many people. Over time, your database will become a professional competitive advantage and a personal electronic soul mate.

Package Yourself on Paper

Package yourself. You are a product and the recruitment materials that you send out are your advertisement. I compare my self-promotion packages to direct-mail campaigns—you know, the mail that either gets tossed or elicits a response. Some direct-mail campaigns are more successful with more pieces in the envelope. Each piece provides another opportunity to sell.

I wanted my mailing package to include a variety of parts to attract a larger audience. Over the years, my packages have generally included five parts: a cover letter, a resume, a projects-completed page, a references and speaker page, and a conference flyer. The resume is a one- or two-page traditional chronological resume. The "consulting and marketing projects completed" page describes five very marketable projects and includes the names of the companies where I did each one. This way, if someone likes the cover letter and the resume, they can read about my experience in more detail. The "references and speaker" page helps me gain credibility. (This is just another use of credentials to gain acceptance.) As my list of speeches grew longer, I dropped the references section but retained the speeches list. The last page of my package is a conference flyer that shows my picture next to an industry guru's picture because we were both keynote speakers. It adds a bit of pizzazz and visual cues. In fact, it was the only page that one senior executive who interviewed me had kept.

I use this package in mailings to recruiters and potential employers. The projects completed and speeches list also can be viewed on my website.

Create a Home Page and Package Yourself Electronically

When I first put my home page on the Web, it didn't generate a lot of e-mail. I didn't have the time to create a marketing plan for it—I figured I would get to that eventually. At the start, it was more important for me to have the home page address on my resume package and the actual pages on my portable PC.

Keeping your home page on your PC enables you to show it in interviews without accessing the Internet. If you're going to portray yourself as a modern executive, this helps. America Online and several other services provide free software that you can download and use to create a home page. You can check out my home page at http://www.juliahartman.com.

Package Your Work and Use It to Gain Control of the Interview Agenda

I purchased a great big black three-ring binder with clear plastic pockets inside. It weighs over six pounds and does not fit in my briefcase. In it, I have samples of everything important that I or my team has done. (Note: I never include confidential material. If anything can even remotely be considered confidential, I white-out the confidential parts and the company names.) When I go to interviews, the first thing I do is slap this down, opened, in front of the decision maker—generally with my poster out face-up. My binder is so big and heavy that this behavior even appears acceptable.

It's a heck of a way to lead into a conversation. If they say, "Take me through your resume." I say, "OK, plus I have lots of samples of my work to show so that you can get a clear idea of my experience." I start at the point in the binder that is most relevant to the position I'm interviewing for. Hit them with the best goods first. It sets a positive foundation for the rest of the interview because your strong points are covered at the start. After they've seen examples of your best work, turn to whatever other parts in the binder will help you. My best first interviews are show-and-tell sessions. After the interviewers see a few things that impress them, they get curious about what else is in that big binder . . . and then you are in control of the interview!

Gain Control of the Telephone Interview Agenda

Many in-person interviews are preceded by a phone interview. These are usually arranged by the assistant of the decision maker. Ask that assistant for a description of the job being offered. Mention that you will fax a few excerpts of your work to the decision maker just before the call. That way you will be able to discuss your work more definitively during the call. The fax should include a cover letter to the interviewer with a few sentences describing each of your attachments. Intriguing one-page presentation excerpts work well as attachments, especially those with wild diagrams that describe the fascinating aspects of these marketable projects.

You have an excellent chance of completely controlling the phone interview agenda by following these steps. The reason is simple. Phone interviews place quite a lot of pressure on the interviewer. This person doesn't know you, can't see you, and yet is supposed to ask you revealing questions. This is difficult for anyone to do. Give him or her an out—fax them fascinating excerpts of your work, which they'll be curious to find out more about

After the discussion about the weather ends, you will start forming a professional bond based on the discussion of your fax. You will present your strengths from the start. Intrigue them but don't tell all. Make sure they want to know more and mention that you have a portfolio of other examples you can present during an in-person meeting.

Toward the end of the phone interview you need to accomplish the following:

■ Address any objections to your candidacy.

■ Arrange an in-person interview date.

■ End the interview on a friendly and positive note.

Ask about objections to your candidacy so that you can fix this situation before it becomes unfixable. You could say: "Is there anything I've said which could preclude me from getting this job?" Give the interviewer permission to be honest with you and address any objections. Then ask, "So when would you like to get together?" Then be sure to do some friendly bonding and express that you are looking forward to meeting him or her!

Create Opportunities to Feed Your Database

After you meet someone, especially someone influential, add him or her to your database and send a note referencing your meeting. During your speeches, ask for business cards from people who want more information. Make personal contact with the press and other influential people at conferences or business meetings. For example, when I'm at a conference or a meeting, I usually take someone's business card and write his or her classification on it. Then I promptly send each person a note that says I enjoyed our chance to meet. I include my card. With a database program, you can create a letter template, pull up everyone you met at the conference, print a personalized letter to each of them, and print labels in less than half an hour.

Use Your Database to Promote Yourself

Send Holiday Cards to Your Best Contacts

If you have the bucks, send your best contacts a custom printed holiday card with your contact information inside. Some greeting card companies, such as Stu Heinecke Creative Services, make customized greeting cards especially designed to help you get meetings with decision makers (for information, call 206-286-8668). I used a custom card to help close a job offer, used a series of cartoons in a fax campaign aimed at a publisher, and used a poster to win over a division president. These cards have always worked!

Publicize Your Career Moves

Every time you change jobs, send a press release or announcement to your best contacts. Although this is obviously self-promotion, I have found that some people regard these announcements as very considerate. For example, recruiters have invested their time in getting to know you; they do not want to lose contact with you simply because you have changed jobs.

Keep a "press" classification in your database that includes the editor of every trade publication in your industry. Every time that you change jobs, send these editors a press release or a note and picture describing your new responsibilities. (Note: you need your supervisor's approval of this tactic.)

Other Ways to Generate Publicity

■ Draft a letter to an important contact in one industry. Then search through your database for everyone else in the industry and customize the letter so that it is relevant to each of them. (It may just mean changing the first line.) This is especially relevant for sales letters because many of the buzzwords are the same within an industry.

■ Write bylined articles for the trade press and include your permanent phone number in the article. One way to get articles published is to write your press contacts about an interesting project you're working on. If they are interested, draft an article, perhaps with input from others at your company. (Note: Run this one by your company's press contact.) Include those who respond to the article in your database.

■ Find opportunities to speak. Talk to your contacts for referrals, especially vendors.

■ Write handwritten thank-you notes on note cards every day. If you can't think of who to thank today, think again. It can be a great way to start out the day.

Promote Yourself Regularly to Recruiters

Contacts and friends are important but sometimes recruiters provide more effective opportunities. I have found that trading the names of recruiters with colleagues is extremely helpful to all parties. Many times friends are at the same level as you are and they tend to know more about job opportunities at that level, not a higher one.

Recruiters have become an important search vehicle for me in the last several years. Some recruiters were referred to me by friends and others responded to mailings I did using the Kennedy Information recruiter list.

It is helpful to understand the two ways that recruiters are paid before deciding how you may want to interact with them. If the recruiter is retained by a client firm to search for an employee, the recruiter is paid by the client firm regardless of whether or not she finds the chosen candidate. The contingency recruiter is only paid by the client firm if he finds the chosen candidate. In both cases, however, the recruiter is paid by the client firm, not you.

Once you send out your resume to a recruiter, there is the unfortunate possibility that they will send it to a possible employer without your permission. (Because of the way that they are paid, this danger is greater with contingency recruiters.) What if a recruiter sends out your resume to numerous firms without your permission while you are contacting these same employers? In this case the employer may think that she will have to pay the contingency recruiter in order to hire you. This makes you more expensive than other candidates and consequently could put you at a disadvantage.

In my earlier recruitment years, with a less competitive resume, this possibility did not concern me. I worked with as many recruiters as possible, whatever the variety. At higher salary levels, and with more competitive job experience, I saw this as a potential problem. Consequently, I continued working with the contingency recruiters I knew and trusted but worked to increase my exposure to more retainer recruiters.

Here are some specific tactics that you can use to develop and maintain a strong network of recruiters:

- Rent a mailing list of recruiters (such as the Kennedy Information list, 800-531-0007) and do a large mailing of your resume. You can select recruiters geographically and by function. I order the pressure-sensitive labels for easy mailing. The number of resumes you mail depends upon the market demand for your skills and your career. I mailed 300 to 500 resumes to a selection of recruiters in my field of marketing, but in hindsight I believe I should have mailed 1,000 to 1,500. Many other skills would require that you mail even greater numbers of resumes. Over the years, the more I used the recruiters list, the better it worked. The response after the third mailing is much better than the first.

- If you're actively looking for a job, ask your friends if you can use their names to meet their recruiters.

- All recruiters who communicate to you should be added to your database. *Cultivate your responders!* This includes all responders to your resume mailings, all that call you from referrals, and those friends' recruiters who seem interested. After doing recruiter mailings for three years, I had seventy-three recruiters in my database. After five years, I had ninety-five, and after six years, I had 131 recruiters in my database. This is a fantastic network. I also mail these people personally addressed cards during the holiday season.

- Send recruiters in your database an updated resume and a personally addressed letter annually even if you're not actively looking for a new job. I usually send an annual mailing in January because they have just gotten my holiday card. Frequency counts in direct mail. It also helps if your holiday card is distinctive.

■ When recruiters call looking to fill a job, always take the time to help them locate a candidate. One day it may be you. If not, it's a simple database search. In my database, I classify anyone who calls me looking for a job as "looking." Recruiters really appreciate this speedy access to names and those contacts looking for a job appreciate the referral. Someday these same contacts may refer you!

■ When contacts call you looking for a job, always take the time to send them your list of recruiters. Encourage them to use your name when speaking to recruiters. Recruiters appreciate referrals and this keeps your name at the forefront of their minds.

■ If a recruiter calls with the most perfect job but you already have a perfect job, try to at least consider the position. Things may look rosy now, but how will they be tomorrow? Even if your current job is truly great, it's still a good idea to interview in order to make new contacts, gain the experience, *and have another job offer on reserve.*

Summary

I built these promotional tactics by looking for jobs. They helped me land lots of offers. But if you're really hungry to move up or out, it's not enough just to accept one job. It's also not practical to assume that you will have just one job—or that you will be able to keep it. Chapter Five provides additional techniques that you can use to keep finding the best job for you.

5

How to Keep Finding the Greatest Job for You

Tactics 14–19:

14. Build your contacts
15. Do lots of different assignments
16. Do your best work
17. Get recommendations
18. Think about what you like to think about
19. Defend your jumps in interviews: Three good responses to common interview objections

t can be a great source of motivation to pursue a single goal. I did that for eleven years because I wanted to become a professional musician. An equally successful strategy is not knowing *exactly* what you want. If you knew *exactly* what you wanted, you might get it—and you'd miss the opportunity to do something better for yourself. As long as you don't know exactly what you want, you can continue wondering. Now I work toward five possible futures, which are all completely different, and I always consider other options. Why limit your future view? You can continue trying different assignments. You can build your contacts and talk to people about your ideas. Pretty soon you'll be heading in an interesting direction. On that road, what you want will change, and it should. The idea is to build your peripheral vision for what you think you like, and then to broaden this vision. Yes, if you don't know exactly what you want, you are continually looking for jobs and yes, this is an excellent way to build your skills and career!

Build Your Contacts

Vendors are a terrific source of industry information and can introduce you to new horizons. Draw them out and find out as much as possible, politely. Ask about mutual contacts who are leaving or taking new jobs. Ask about your competitors—what are they doing that's new in your industry?

Industry gurus are another source of great information. I have sometimes run across assignments that only an industry guru could figure out. These people like the tough assignments and enjoy being solicited for their opinions.

The *trade press* know all sides of the issues and can lend great perspective on your assignment. They are readily available at conferences and online. However, when dealing with the press, remember to exercise caution in your own online dialogue because it may interfere with company policies at work. (Other techniques for building contacts were discussed in Chapter Four.)

Do Lots of Different Assignments

One of the reasons that I went to Citibank after I got my MBA is that they had a training program where you designed your own rotations. I had never worked in a big company before and had no idea if I might be interested in finance, treasury, retail branches, strategic planning, or something else. I knew that I liked marketing but didn't really know what the other fields entailed. These rotations broadened my understanding of marketing as well as the other fields. Consulting and contracted employee assignments at other firms also enabled me to try many different types of projects. By taking on many different types of assignments, I gained a broad and tactical understanding of the marketing profession. This foundation of knowledge gave me the confidence to forge my own career directions.

Do Your Best Work

When I was studying violin, I said to my teacher, "I want to learn the Beethoven violin concerto." His response was: "You will *not* learn the Beethoven violin concerto. You must learn that it is not *what* you play but *how* you play that matters. The Beethoven violin concerto is too advanced for your skills, but you will learn to play the Adagio in E major by Mozart superbly!" I had to take his advice because it took me years of practice to learn that piece to the best of my ability. I did not have the time to do something poorly. After a while I became thrilled at playing well, doing the best I possibly could, regardless of the assignment.

If you're working in a position that systematically prevents you from doing your best, either change this circumstance or say good-bye to the company. If you're not doing your best work, you are limiting yourself and your employer. It's not worth your time and it probably isn't worth your employer's time either. Your creative skills will deteriorate and, if you're like me, you may gain a few unwanted pounds.

I once interviewed with a traditional "old school" insurance company. They told me exactly what they wanted done. I thought their plan was antiquated, a poor use of resources, and boring. (Their plan was much worse than this but I will refrain from further comment.) As the interview progressed, the senior vice president said, "It's not *what* you do, but *who* you do it for." Obviously, this had worked for him; he was an SVP. However, simply following plans that I feel are ineffective doesn't work for me. I have to feel passionate about what I do. If I realize that I'm not doing it for the right person, then I'll go get a new supervisor. That senior vice president might be chairman of his company some day. But I might too, and I'll get there my way! Life is too short not to enjoy it.

Get Recommendations

When you do your best work for an industry guru be sure to ask them if they would recommend you to other employers. In the earlier stages of my career, I listed their names and positions as recommendations on the recommendations and speeches page of my recruitment package. These provided credibility, opened doors, and shortened time in negotiating offers. As you obtain more senior positions, it may not be necessary to include these in your package; just keep them on reserve for references.

Think About What You Like to Think About

This is an essential step. It's important to be extremely comfortable with your thoughts, your mental life. If something is getting you down, get it out of your head. If some thought is lifting you up, linger on that one and the next one. . . . While you're building your contacts and trying lots of different assignments, be sure to notice what you like and gravitate toward it.

I've been through a career change and changed jobs a lot and I've often tried to do the exercises in the self-help books. I thought these exercises would help me decide what I wanted to do. Unfortunately, the ones I tried were not fun so I couldn't use them. Instead, what works for me is to do lots of different assignments and get lots of input from people. I need time to reflect on these experiences and then the freedom to make changes in my situation.

Defend Your Jumps in Interviews: Three Good Responses to Common Interview Objections

Objection: I suppose you don't get emotionally attached to any company because you change jobs so much.

Answer: I get very passionately involved with every job. That's because when I choose a job it is exactly what I want to be doing. I have made a conscious choice to immerse myself in a particular company at a particular time doing a particular assignment. This assignment is the direction I am choosing for my career. You can see how the previous assignments led up to this one. (Show examples from your resume.) This is exactly what I want to do and I'm very excited about the opportunity here.

Objection: Why did you leave *x* job?

Answer: In the course of showing the interviewer your promotional portfolio (see page 47) you should proactively explain why you left each job. This has got to be smoothly worded and practiced ahead of time. There should be a positive reason why you left each job and why the next job was the right fit. If there was a reorganization and you were laid off, just say so—this is very common and if you don't say it, the perception will be that you jumped more often than you actually did. Here are some of the reasons I provided in job interviews for why I left particular companies for other jobs:

- I saw the reorganization coming and I had the opportunity to double my salary in just one consulting assignment.
- A competitor bought me.
- I went back to the client side because after working for many of the major vendors in the field I had gained the skills to run the entire function, not just a part of it.
- Our department reported to six managers in the course of a year. Although I did the job I was hired to do (give examples), the company's commitment to direct and database marketing was not growing quickly enough to satisfy my abilities in this field. This turmoil of senior management prevented quick growth of this function and I was only willing to grow it quickly.

HOW TO KEEP FINDING THE GREATEST JOB FOR YOU

Objection: It looks like you've worked for a lot of different companies.

Answer: I have, but as you can see from my resume, many of the assignments were for a contracted period; both the employer and myself agreed upon the assignment and length of employment up front. At times my contracts were as an independent consultant with no health benefits and other times I was a contracted employee with benefits. Actually some people look upon my exposure to many companies as a strength. One employer remarked that because I had been hired by most of the major vendors in the industry, then I had to have the skills needed to do the job.

Summary

It's quite empowering to use the tactics discussed in this chapter to keep finding the best job for yourself. But then another question arises: What's the optimum speed with which to jump jobs? That depends upon your preferences and the acceptability of jumping jobs in your particular field—topics explained in the next chapter.

Perspectives on Jumping from Recruiters, Human Resource Professionals, and an Entrepreneur

Topics:

■ When are jumpers easy to market and when are they difficult?

■ Do employers look for people who have remained at one company for a certain length of time?

■ When someone has been laid off or fired, what is the best way for them to describe this to you?

■ What do you do with unsolicited materials from candidates? How important is a referral? How important is the cover letter?

■ Perspectives and advice on jumping

s there a stigma to jumping? If you're a jumper, how often is too often to make a jump? You may be having thoughts like: "How acceptable is it to change jobs? How will this jump affect my reputation in the future? How many other professionals are changing jobs? What is an acceptable tenure in a job today?" This chapter reviews opinions ranging from very conservative to very liberal. The answers below somewhat reflect supply and demand and also reflect how the respondent is employed.

Let's look at the supply-and-demand approach. Everybody knows that certain types of computer programmers are in hot demand. These programmers can go from job to job and face no stigma for it; people are used to it and work with it. I've also seen this with other skill sets. In other words, the more marketable your skills are, the more acceptable it is to jump. (Another conclusion could be that as more functions become contract jobs, jumping will become more commonplace.)

How do you gauge the acceptability factor? How do you know if you will face a stigma for jumping? You need to find out where your skills lie in the supply–demand spectrum so that you can see how acceptable jumping is in your industry. A practical approach is to compare your skills and career with a group of colleagues. Among your colleagues, how long, on average, are they staying in each job? If you have the same skills but you jump more often than the average of this group, you may face more of a stigma then they will. Your references may be among this group of colleagues. Would you still be able to count on them as references if you did jump?

Another way to gauge the situation is to ask what your options would be if you lost your new job after being there for only a short time. Would it appear to be a short jump in a series? Can you afford to have a series of jumps? Another gauge is recruiters. Is the pace of calls from recruiters increasing or decreasing for you? Call a few who know you well and ask when your career would be enhanced by another jump.

You may face a stigma for jumping with certain employers but not others. In addition to supply-and-demand considerations, job seekers should keep in mind how the interviewer is employed. Is the interviewer a recruiter or an employer? Recruiters are employed by their client companies. If the recruiter's clients tend to look for traditional "loyal" employees, that recruiter may find jumpers less marketable. If the recruiter's clients are more open-minded, then that recruiter may have a more positive opinion of jumpers.

To gain a fuller perspective on the question of jumping, I asked recruiters, outplacement professionals, human resource professionals, and an entrepreneur for their opinions and advice. In some cases, last names are abbreviated to protect identity. This is *not* a scientific survey, but it does provide insights to the questions posed above and includes many different perspectives.

When Are Jumpers Easy to Market and When Are They Difficult?

Ralph Peragine, Managing Partner, and Ward Perrott, Vice President, The Resource Group (exclusively retained searches):

We try to determine whether candidates have made intelligent moves throughout their career. We've always frowned upon people making moves strictly for dollars and not opportunity. We should see moves toward growth as far as responsibility, title, and type of company. To explain this person's background to a potential hiring company, there have to be sound, logical business reasons for making changes—hopefully positive reasons.

John T., Vice President, Large Recruitment Firm (exclusively retained searches):

The predominant rationale has to be that there was some common thread in what these people were doing, either functionally or experientially or in an entrepreneurial way. I just ran into this. A client initially rejected a candidate who had three entrepreneurial companies in a row. Then he went back to a larger company, left there after a year and a half, and went to a consulting firm. He had six jobs in nine years. They initially rejected his candidacy. Then I went back to them and said, "Look, understand what this person was doing. This person was trying to grab a brass ring. Each of these three entrepreneurial roles ultimately failed but that's not to say that he didn't have the courage to go after them. What it in fact shows is that this person has courage as opposed to being a flake." In each instance I was able to prove through references that he added significant value—but it took time.

There are two factors mitigating against presenting someone like that in my business. One is the search person has to believe in this person pretty heavily to invest the time in order to persuade the client to go further. The other is that it's very difficult for a client to get over job-hopping because they're investing say $50,000 or more in my fee and they are potentially going to invest a significant amount of money relocating this person. They have a company that they have to run and they need consistent leadership. They're concerned that this person isn't going to stay more than two years or maybe less.

As the recruiter, you have to believe that the candidate is looking at this as being a longer-term opportunity for various reasons. One is entrepreneurial enough: "There's stock options here even though it's not the brass ring I was going for. Or: I'm really tired of job-hopping, I've done my bit, I've got a family to raise, I like this intellectually and forget making $1 million. I'll stay."

Charles Baker, Vice President, Marc Nichols Associates (contingency and retainer recruitment firm):
The candidate is easy to market when he or she is really outstanding. If they go from their first job to their third job fairly

quickly but they're also moving up very quickly as opposed to making almost lateral moves, then you know there's something special there. In order to do this moving around and be successful at it, you've got to have that extra zing, that extra special factor. Some people just move, move, move . . . and they're nice, relatively smart, fairly attractive, and personable. But if you're not a superstar or don't have the makings of a superstar after a very short period of time, then it's going to come to a screeching halt and you're going to get in trouble.

Chris Mangieri, President, Mangieri Solutions (contingency and retainer recruitment firm):

It depends on the reasons that the candidate made each change. Many times in this day and age you'll see lots of things on the resume but it's no fault of their own. You'll see they've had three jobs in a row where they've been there a year and the position's been eliminated or the company's been sold. Job-hopping is not as much of a stigma as it used to be. In fact now it's almost gone the reverse. If you stay at one company too long, you're suspect.

If you're working with a Fortune 500 company that still has that tradition of people there twenty and thirty years, sometimes a number of jumps may hurt you. If you're dealing with a very young, entrepreneurial upstart company, then they don't care. They ask, "What have you done for your past employers? How can you do it for me?" There're no hard and fast rules about this anymore. You know ten, fifteen, twenty years ago there were. If you jumped around a lot, nobody wanted you. The world has changed. The security risks that were inherent in going to a small company are no longer a disadvantage. There's no job security anywhere anymore.

Don Noble, President, Noble & Associates
(contingency and retainer recruitment firm):
They're easier to market if many of their job changes came earlier rather than later in their careers. They're easier to market if there's some rhyme or reason to why these folks made a move—they went to a better company, they had expanded responsibilities, that kind of thing. They are more difficult to market if they haven't really spent very much time in each company and they can't give logical reasons for the jumps. In this marketplace as opposed to ten years ago, it's understandable that people move jobs. There's never been as much downsizing in the past as there is today. Even the people that are left suddenly have workloads that they never had before. Some of their additional work is doing menial things that used to be done by other people. That's a reason to move. People move because of money, because of geographical location, and for personal reasons. It's much more acceptable today that people move. But there comes a point in time when you've got to light in a place, and when you do that you've got to be there long enough to accept responsibility.

Do Employers Look for People Who Have Remained at One Company for a Certain Length of Time?

Pat Dowd, President, Pat Dowd Inc.
(retained and contingency searches):
When they have stayed somewhere at least three, preferably four years after they've jumped around, they've showed stabil-

ity. That's the first thing some hiring authorities notice in a resume. As the recruiter, you have to be ready for it. There are good reasons for moving around. I look at what the person can do. Can they do the job? That's the most important thing.

Ralph Peragine and Ward Perrott:

Generally most job descriptions state the number of years of required experience. Many companies like to see a three- to five-year tenure with a firm. The opposite situation is that when somebody has stayed with a company for too long, the potential employer questions, "Why hasn't this person made a move? Why hasn't someone been able to attract them or why haven't they sought out a different balance in their career?"

Don Noble:

I think employers today like to see more of a variety of experience. Although they don't state this, they seem to be more comfortable when the candidate has stayed with a company at least three years. However, employers are always suspicious if a person's been at one company their whole career—unless they've had a meteoric rise to the top and they're moving because they're blocked at a top tier.

Chris Mangieri:

It's rare that anyone mentions that to me anymore. It used to be you wouldn't even send a resume of somebody that's job-hopped a lot and now it's really a non-issue.

Charles Baker:

Companies don't ask for it but a few stints of two to three years each will fly. If you start seeing a lot of one-year stints, and especially if you see periods where they were a "consultant" or periods of unemployment, then those people become very suspect.

When People Have Been Laid Off or Fired, What Is the Best Way for Them to Describe This to You?

I'd quote individual answers for you here, but in all cases the recruiters wanted honesty. They stressed that downsizing is common and if that happened just say so. They want to know the circumstances of the situation. Recruiters can also find out the truth by checking references and talking to peers.

What Do You Do with Unsolicited Materials from Candidates? How Important Is a Referral? How Important Is the Cover Letter?

Most recruiters mentioned that all resumes, regardless of whether they are solicited or not, are reviewed to ascertain if the person has skills in the industries for which they are recruiting. In some firms, the resume is scanned into a database and candidates' skills are coded.

Here is how Steve Schwartz, vice president, Management Recruiters of Grammercy, described their coding system: "We code our applicants in any number of different ways including education, geographic preference, industry preference, title, years of experience, salary levels, and preferences in terms of size of company, but at some point in time the human factor has to come in." Coding systems enable the recruiter to source all the candidates within their database who have a particular group of skills.

Most recruiters said that referrals are very important. For some, referrals are their largest source of candidates. Many recruiters said that they read the cover letter very carefully for various reasons, such as geographical preference or to see a writing sample. Others said that they do not read the cover letter.

Perspectives and Advice on Jumping

Ralph Peragine and Ward Perrott:

Before candidates make job changes, they need to consider the emotional aspect of the change. People change jobs for emotional reasons and then rationalize that it's a business decision. Most of what they deal with is the emotionalism, whether it be leaving the company, leaving an area, leaving their family, changing friends, and things to that effect. There are emotional things that come into job changes that sometimes people don't really take into consideration until the very end.

Pat Dowd:

Be very careful about which companies you choose along the way. They have to be blue-chip companies in terms of the product or the service. They've got to be the best company in the industry. They've got to be a top company and a generic household word. They can't be unknown entities. If somebody in a high-caliber company hires you, there has to be a reason. Be sure that you've researched whether they're going to be acquired, whether you really know the company walking in.

Another word of advice is to be nice to your recruiter. You want to be eager to help because that person's going to remember you more than somebody that's got your resume sitting in the file and that you never hear from. When you make your move, the more professional candidates make an announcement in a letter that describes their new position and gives their new phone number and address. The least professional candidates don't even let anybody know they've moved. They get lost and the relationship that they had with the recruiter is gone when they move from one job to another.

Chris Mangieri:

If you're considering changing jobs, my advice is to look at the opportunity in the short term. Don't look at it as much in the long term anymore. What valuable experience are you going to get? Don't just look at the money issue. Sometimes I talk to people who just look at the money. In all reality, it's a nice bump but it's not going to change your lifestyle. What will really allow you to grow and expand your opportunities and enable you to move into different facets and more interesting opportunities? Money is not the most important factor. Unless you're jumping up 100 percent, it's not going to change your lifestyle.

John T.:

If you're going to have job-hopping as a strategy, two things come to mind: Give up hierarchical notions of success and save money. Look at success as a series of satisfactory projects which you completed and which made a difference. Then move on. In today's world, don't expect to have a major operational role in the company. That may change down the road because temporary services are growing. Eventually you could be a contract employee, which is normally a functional situation—a good programmer, a good accountant.

The other side of it is that unless you have a skill set that sells for a fair amount of money on the open market as a consultant, it would never be a way to amass significant wealth. Consultants can build wealth because they can charge high fees for what they do. A worker who job hops is just another individual in the company with a title and role and will not be paid the premium that temporary high level consulting work gets paid.

You have to be willing to live with those trade-offs for the satisfaction of your work. You have to be very strong and secure personally to do this. If you have a spouse, he or she has to feel the same way.

Charles Baker:

The people who are going to be successful jumping jobs often are in the top 10 percent of the job pool. These are the superstars. They're going to do this and do it well. Quite frankly, most of us drones have to stick to the usual procedures and the usual time frames. That's a ticklish subject but I think it's the way of the world.

Susan Rietano Davey, Partner, Flexible Resources:

We champion flexibility in the workplace. Professionals can work in alternate locations on flexible schedules and be as productive as those who work in traditional locations with traditional hours. Our candidates include corporate executives, consultants, and retirees who, for a number of reasons, want to work outside a normal schedule. We market their talent and expertise to companies that will hire them on their preferred schedule.

FRI clients run the gamut of large and small companies, in a variety of industries, and include Nabisco, General Electric, and United Technologies. Our placements are 50 percent permanent and 50 percent temporary or "contract." Contract assignments can run from four months to two years, in such disciplines as human resources, information technology, finance, and marketing. Clients pay us a 25 percent commission on the wage paid to the employee for up to twelve months or, if headcount issues exist, can pay an additional 15 percent surcharge to have us payroll the candidate ourselves.

Albert C. Shuckra, Career Consultant, Drake Beam Morin, Inc.:

People who are looking for a job tend to land one faster if they can visualize the job they want and if they can capture their past experience in accomplishment statements. One individual I worked with took three weeks and made a very comprehensive list of all the characteristics of her ideal job. This was not the specific type of work that she wanted but instead the atmosphere in which she would be working. She answered questions like: "What kind of people would I be working with? What would the environment be? What's the culture like? What kind of contact would I have with people? What would the boss be like?" She visualized the characteristics of her ideal job—not the title or the function but the atmosphere. I have found that in her case and in many others, once you have the concept of your ideal job you are more receptive to spotting these opportunities.

The next step is networking and determining where these ideal job characteristics exist in a real job. Ask your contacts where you would find these elements. Look in the *Dictionary of Occupational Titles* published by the U.S. Department of Labor. It has detailed descriptions of 40,000 jobs.

Candidates move through the job search process faster when they can capture their past experience in accomplishment statements. What did they do for their employers to create economic value? Here's an example from someone who had a position in the insurance industry in auto and real estate property claims: He developed and implemented national strategic initiatives and vendor alliances, which saved his company over $500,000 in the costs to purchase glass products. Now this candidate can say, "I did this and can do the same thing for you."

Tom L., Entrepreneur:

I believe that the days of long-term employment with any given company are no longer a viable career path. I really feel that job-jumping benefits both the person and the company. I personally have never looked at somebody's resume and said, "Boy this person has left every job in two years and that's a detriment." In most cases, I have found people who jump jobs to be a lot more open-minded, to be a lot more aggressive, and to be more well-rounded than people who've sat in the same company for twenty years. I've hired these jumpers and I've found that they bring more to the party. As an employer, I've been in situations where some of my people felt that this person's had too many jobs and that that was a negative. I looked at it and felt that it was more of a positive.

I believe that you don't have to stay in the same job for five or ten years to understand how to do that job. We're in a much faster paced world, so that progress up the organization doesn't exist. Your progress is dependent upon your career moves, which expand your horizons. The day that you start feeling complacent and that you've learned and contributed everything you can in a job, is the day that you probably ought to move on. With today's environment, practically speaking, it is much more lucrative to move on even if you do the same job someplace else. The more you learn, the more you earn. Jumping allows you to do both.

Also, I think there's a ceiling with where you can go with jobs in the same company. If people are already "in place" in certain positions, you can't move up unless they leave. Jumpers don't wait for the opportunity, they create their own.

In summary, jumping is a win–win for everyone and I respect both the jumpers and those employers who are willing to hire them. Jumpers are the "fire in the belly" of tomorrow's businesses.

Summary

It's my opinion that the supply and demand of your skills is the primary factor that determines the acceptability of your job jumps. If you think your skills are more competitive than your peers, you can be handsomely rewarded for jumping.

But part of the game today is inventing the rewards, a topic that is explored in Chapter Seven.

7

Get Paid
Coming
and Going

Tactics 20–27:
20. 'Tis the season to be paid!
21. Three ways to get a signing bonus
    (dialogues #1 and #2)
22. Reengineer more for you: Profit from
    restructuring
23. Company being sold? Get paid
24. Exit bonuses: Obtain sever-thyself payments
    (dialogue #3)
25. Exit bonuses: Up your severance
    (dialogue #4)
26. Resignation payments and exit bonuses for
    salespeople (dialogue #5)
27. Double-whammy opportunities:
    Simultaneous bonuses

W e work in very turbulent times. You can either learn how to benefit from this new environment or be victimized by it. Executives now have a special window of opportunity to negotiate lots of different types of bonuses. Jumpers are not limited to the staid annual bonuses that are usually part and parcel of executive packages. Incentive compensation is very popular. In addition, some jumpers negotiate special "sugar lumps" for coming and going: signing bonuses and exit bonuses. Signing bonuses lure attractive candidates and exit bonuses reward these same people.

In salary negotiations, you may find it effective to memorize exactly what you want to say. This type of conversation requires complete confidence and clarity in your own point of view. Rehearse your speech with your spouse or a friend. Rehearse answers to the expected objections. Write out an outline of key points or the script. Be ready at least a week in advance of your meeting . . . and remember, sometimes you are not in control of the meeting date.

As contract and incentive compensation become popular tools to retain employees, occurrences of signing, exit, and annual bonuses will decrease. As more individuals negotiate contract and incentive employment, it becomes less competitive for employers to offer ambiguous bonuses. Instead, if employers put all the compensation into the contracts, they can offer positions that are more competitive because they have a higher upside.

Currently, widespread acceptance of contract employment has not yet happened. Employers are in a compromised situation—they recognize the risks that candidates take by jumping jobs and they realize that with downsizing, reengineering, and so on their job offer may be somewhat tenuous. Many have not yet discovered the business value of retaining key employees. Employees question whether it is worthwhile to stay at such a firm. Consequently, at this time, bonuses abound; there are literally bonuses for just about all seasons. . . .

'Tis the Season to Be Paid!

January to March
When does your current company pay bonuses? If they announce bonuses in December but pay sometime in the spring,

you might lose your bonus if you leave early in the first quarter. This is a reason to negotiate a signing bonus at your new firm and then to negotiate a severance at your old firm. January is also a good month for new beginnings, for lagging negotiations to really gain strength and come to fruition.

April to June

The second quarter does not strike me as having any special negotiation advantages. If you are looking for a new job in this quarter, you'd better hurry up because the summer slows down with people on vacation.

July to September

July and August can be slow but September is like January, a month of new beginnings. Everybody has just gotten back from summer vacation and is raring to go. The second week of September is a good time to have your resume on the decision makers' desks. If you've got kids in school, July and August are the last months you can be hired without disrupting their school year. You don't want them to attend two schools in one school year, right? Anybody would understand that. So, if you're negotiating in July and August, this time-frame consideration may help close the deal.

October to December

The bonuses rap from the first quarter may apply; that is, you may have the opportunity to negotiate an exit bonus in lieu of your year-end bonus as well as a signing bonus at your new firm. There is a slowdown during the holidays, but an increased effort to get things done before then. Even if you

---

A Contest: Calling All Employment-Negotiation Dialogues

Before we delve into my actual experiences in employment negotiations, I'd like to mention this: the best way to learn about negotiation dialogues is by sharing our collective experiences. This chapter contains $82,000 worth of bonus dialogue verbiage, all of which lasted less than an hour total when used for bonus discussions with several firms. You probably know of other similar stories.

I am sponsoring an ongoing contest for the best employment-negotiation dialogues. I will post some of these stories on the Internet and offer a free *Strategic Job Jumping* book to each of the top twenty dialogues. Couldn't you use an extra copy for a friend? E-mail your dialogues to:

jh@juliahartman.com

If you win, you will be contacted. If you want anonymity, you've got it. Of course, it's understood that your dialogue could end up on the Internet or in my next book.

---

doubt that negotiations will conclude by the holidays, the company's desire to get them done before the holidays begin may give your negotiations a boost. In addition, there is pressure from some corporate budgets to fill positions before the end of the year.

Three Ways to Get a Signing Bonus

Dialogue #1

$10,000

In some cases, it's as simple as asking for one. The first time that I asked for a signing bonus was an easy negotiation. I simply tacked on an innocent question when the decision maker and I were discussing compensation: ". . . and does this position include a signing bonus?" After some hesitation she said yes and later on we agreed on $10,000.

Dialogue #2

$15,000

I negotiated my second signing bonus with a direct-marketing organization which claimed that it wanted to invest millions and grow extremely quickly. However, the interviewing and negotiation process had already taken close to four months. Finally I said, "Your first-year guarantee is not really competitive with my current position. The longer we drag this out, the more I'm concerned that your firm is not serious about really revving up your business quickly. If you're serious about this, you need to show me that you're serious about me. I need to feel that you have invested in me from day one. Call it a signing bonus or call it a relocation bonus, call it anything, but if you could bring that first-year guarantee up to x by including this bonus, your offer would be more competitive." I asked for more than I thought I'd get and they came back and offered me half of it, $15,000, the next day.

The Spreadsheet Approach

A third way to get a signing bonus is a spreadsheet approach. After receiving an offer, executives provide their recruiters with printouts of all the different potential components of the compensation. Blank spaces show when requests are not being satisfied. As the blank spaces become more numerous, and the requests more detailed, some companies try to fill in the blanks by offering a lump sum to cover several considerations.

Reengineer More for You— Profit from Restructuring

Have you ever been on the receiving end of the restructuring of your organization? I was never up in the ivory tower figuring out the new floors everyone was going to work on. But I must say, when I was out in the field, I never once got a memo stating what the outcome goals of the restructuring effort would be. I never got a one-pager that said, "As a result of our restructuring effort, we are going to increase return on x investment x percent by x date." Does figuring out "better" processes really matter if there are no published and agreed-upon outcomes and no dates upon which to measure this performance?

Unless you're running it, today's "slash-and-burn" restructuring means you must get your resume out there immediately and plaster the market with it. Get out there ahead of the restructuring and develop lots of options for yourself, externally as well as internally, if you're interested in staying. Restructuring means uncertainty. Any environment that had a quasi meritocracy might now have King Kong dangling small people outside skyscraper windows. There's also a chance the whole thing won't matter. In this case you can tell all your new offers, "No thanks, guys, we've just restructured and we're feeling great!" Or, you may find something more comfortable and sensible elsewhere.

Management consultants have criticized restructuring efforts for strategic reasons. Oftentimes restructuring doesn't increase the productivity of the company. A lot of them don't attempt to transform the future of the industry. Some of the key problems in handling the personal side of restructuring are business concerns as well:

Personal Uncertainty. What's going to happen to me? We've just heard an ax is about to fall.... Could you please mention the date? When is it going to happen? You never get a decent amount of time to figure out your next move.

Ability to Participate in the Change. If you really think you know what should be done in the restructuring, you may not have the opportunity to express it to anyone that can help you change the organization. If you're not in the group that is changing the company; your ideas do not get considered.

While we are on the topic of restructuring, may I ask your opinion? If you've been through restructuring, what do you think of this approach for the future? What if the company announces a restructuring effort and simultaneously provides a fixed-length employment contract to all employees of the affected areas and ground rules like these:

■ Anyone's contract can be renewed according to the terms of the contract. Perhaps each contract could come up for renewal a quarter of the way through, halfway through, and three-quarters of the way through. That means that if you have a one-year contract you have three chances during the year to have it renewed: after three months, after six months, and after nine months. The renewal contract could be for a longer or shorter time period and could be for more or less pay. For example a star performer might negotiate a two-year renewal contract for 30 percent more pay, after working three months under the original contract. If the company is trying to change, why not first reward the people that can figure out their role in effecting the change? This sends the right message to the rest of the employees—that is, you will be rewarded if you take a role in changing the company.

■ Anyone can provide plans for restructuring the organization, his job, or his function.

■ Anyone can present these plans in open company meetings.

■ Your current boss may not be your future boss. Anyone may present her plans to the group overseeing the restructuring.

Michael McGowan, senior vice president and general manager of a major temporary staffing company, says, "We are all temporary employees." If you experience a restructuring, you may come to agree with him. However, it seems to me that the use of contract employment in this situation would get everyone to cooperate as quickly as possible and would also give individuals a better way to plan their destiny.

Another advantage employees have with a contract is that it is no longer a "sin" to be recruiting elsewhere. If an employee feels that he could be laid off literally at any moment, his company is not promoting loyalty! In a restructuring situation, many employees are recruiting externally anyway. With contract employment, employees can finally publicly recruit externally— and they should! Contract employment actually benefits all parties. Employers are obviously looking to shed employees and contracts can help them do it. Contracts can also help them retain key employees.

Sometimes frontline and lower-level employees are not given a forum to provide input to the restructuring. Here's what Gary Hamel, an influential strategist and co-author of *Competing for the Future* (Harvard Business School Press, 1994) said about this in a *Business Week* article: "You have to bring in new voices to the process. I find it amazing that young people who live closest to the future are the most disenfranchised in most strategy-creating exercises" ("Strategic Planning," *Business Week*, 8/26/96).

Company Being Sold? Get Paid

Back to the present. Practically speaking, if your company is being sold, get your resume out there as soon as this is announced. Better yet, if you think that the rumors are true, get your paperwork out *before* it's announced.

If your company announces, as one of mine did, that they are *simultaneously being sold and doing a corporate-wide reengineering effort, you have every reason to go on a time-consuming personal crusade throughout your entire industry to find the best job for yourself.* In times of ambiguity, your biggest strength is having choices. You owe it to your future to develop the best possible choices for yourself.

Exit Bonuses: Obtain Sever-Thyself Payments

Some jumpers negotiate exit payments when they are leaving their jobs, although this is risky. Some jumpers, generally those at very high management levels, negotiate severance contracts when they are being hired. Some negotiate guaranteed annual bonuses that double as severance payments if need be. Others negotiate exit bonuses when the company is reengineered, when they are laid off, or when they leave a sales position.

I've volunteered for severance and preceded mass severances, I've been laid off and outcast, and I've resigned when I was a star. But I was paid each time. This is the life of a corporate vagabond. According to *Sports Illustrated,* eight out of ten Americans will be fired at least once (Harvey Mackay, *Sharkproof,* HarperBusiness, 1993). If it hasn't yet happened to you, you might as well look forward to the excitement! You will always remember these special moments and how you handled them. *The point is not what the company thinks of you, but what you think of yourself.*

My feeling is that exit payments are simply there for the taking. The current policy of paying severance primarily for job discontinuance is unfair and arbitrary. If the company pays unequal exit payments for any reason, the de facto policy is . . . *get yours!*

If you see the handwriting on the wall—such as 25 percent of your department is going to get laid off—you had better develop some external options. You may fear that your company will find out that you are recruiting. Don't worry about this too much. Generally, in this type of climate, *everyone* is recruiting. Consequently it's not a likely reason to be terminated. In this type of situation, I've been discreet but complete. I've sent out lots of resumes and I've been ready with other offers before the layoffs started.

Sometimes it's better to go first. Companies have a way of changing their severance policies (downward) before mass layoffs. If you ever find out that the severance policy will change in a few months, you had better aim to have offers in hand before the policy changes. Below is my "sever-thyself" conversation with the human resources of *ABC* company. I was within the first 10 percent to go and all but 15 percent of the department was laid off within a year. I ended up with a $25,000 lump sum severance payment and accepted a consulting assignment days later, an offer that doubled my *ABC* company salary.

Dialogue #3

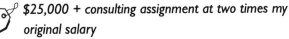

$25,000 + consulting assignment at two times my original salary

Me: Thanks for taking the time to meet with me today.

H.R.:   It's great to see you. What's up?

Me: I was wondering if we could review the current severance policy and compare that to the new one coming up.

H.R.:   . . . err, uh . . . hmm . . . I don't know if I really have this information.

Me: Well we really don't need to know the broad-based policy. I'm just trying to figure out how it would affect me, in my current salary and grade.

H.R.:   OK, I can look up some of those figures. Now what level are you at? This is about what it is now, and that could decrease to about *x*, later.

Me: Wow! That's quite a great package now. I'd hate to get the new one.

H.R.:   Well we have no idea anyway if anyone will get laid off.

93

Me: Well, thanks a lot for the information! Let me know if you get any news.

H.R.: Of course I will, and remember that everyone will be treated with the utmost dignity and respect. (Don't you love that phrase?)

A few days later, the department head offered me the option to switch to another job within the company, or get a lump-sum severance payment. Strangely enough, my immediate supervisor did not know that I was in the process of being transferred or laid off. When I told him the news, he was furious about how he and I were being treated.

I could have gotten the same salary at other jobs within the company but there wasn't one I was truly excited about. I loved this supervisor and this job. We were in the middle of fantastically interesting projects, we were learning a great deal, and we had a great working relationship. Then a strange thought occurred to me: If this firm needs to reduce its head count (on paper) why didn't I just switch sides? I could have the same supervisor and job if he agreed to fund a fixed-term consulting contract with a vendor. I went to him with this idea and he agreed to this incredible plan.

Thus, by becoming a contractor, I ended up working for two companies simultaneously at twice my previous salary plus the $25,000 severance fee! On the vendor side, I gained a new boss and office, as well as sales and consulting assignments. On the client side, I kept my office at firm *ABC*, kept the same job responsibilities, which I enjoyed, and still reported to the same supervisor. It was a crazy but happy situation. I had now become a consultant and I loved every minute of it.

Exit Bonuses: Up Your Severance

Layoffs happen. I've gotten laid off too. Before we explore how I extricated myself, you might be interested in finding out more about a place where I once worked—you may know it!

I worked in a massive architecturally award-winning suburban office park, which employed over 5,000 people. My building was a huge, high, glass-and-steel structure which was so modern that I had a hard time getting my bearings. All the floors looked so similar and the basement-level corridors were truly a maze. During my first month on the job, I had a terrifying experience. I became enthralled in my work, stayed late, and by the time I was ready to go home, everyone else had left. I got lost on the premises while trying to leave the building to get to my car. I became confused in the lower-level maze and took an exit that led to a huge field and woods. There was no parking lot in sight but I was scared to stay in that eerie basement maze—the different-colored locked doors, the large pipes, the strange corners! While hiking around in my dress shoes in the dark, I found the entrance to another building and got in through my card key. Thank goodness there was a phone inside. I called security. They picked me up in a car and drove me to my car—which was at least a mile away. I thought that I was truly saved!

Unfortunately, I also got lost a few times while going to work in the morning. I had no trouble driving to the complex, but once inside my building, I sometimes mistakenly got off the elevator on the wrong floor. I found huge areas where the lights were on, the cubes, computers, and phones were there, but the desks were totally empty! I would think that I was on my floor but that all the people had disappeared. When I finally made it to my desk and asked about these other floors, I was told all about it: "Oh yes, we outsourced that function last week and those people were all let go."

Strangely enough, this experience happened several times. Then one day it happened again but I wasn't on the wrong floor. . . .

A short while later, my time had come to get laid off. But I can look back at it positively because I was extremely ready to be laid off. I was in the process of negotiating an external offer. I had been rehearsing my exit speech with my husband for at least two weeks. As soon as I got the ax, I unleashed the speech, immediately, without a minute to spare. Sometimes it is important to do your exit speech immediately. Your bargaining position may be strongest, and his the weakest, at the very moment he tells you the news. He wants to end this awkward meeting as soon as possible, *even if he has to pay to end it.* Plus he's prepared to deal with an employee who's paralyzed into submission by the surprise of this awful news.

In my case, he was shocked by my speech. He didn't face a paralyzed executive; I was totally ready to make the most of the experience. In one fifteen-minute conversation, I upped the severance from two weeks to three months—a $22,000 lump-sum payment. I also accepted a more competitive external offer a few days later, just before I left.

Dialogue #4

$22,000

Me: I saw your note [to drop by his office]. What's up?

Ted: Oh, Julia, I've been wanting to meet with you. Have a seat. It's about your position. You know we've had to cut expenses and . . . I'm sorry, we had to eliminate your position.

Me: Really?

Ted: Yes. I know you're upset but we have an outplacement service in the other building and all our policies are included in this package right here.

Me: Thank you. Is there a severance provision in this package?

Ted: Of course, it's all in there. I'm sure you'll need some time to read it over and Miss Jones is ready to answer any questions you may have.

Me: That's very helpful. I appreciate that, Ted. So how much is the severance?

Ted: Oh I don't know, I'm sure it's in there somewhere.

Me: Well, let's find it. If we look through these papers I'm sure it will be spelled out.

Ted: . . . ah OK, all right, here it is . . . two weeks' severance.

Me: Two weeks!? Ted, do you really think that's fair? Let's review this situation. *ABC* company relocated me here from New York City. My husband quit his job and became a consultant to allow me to take this job. Three weeks after I arrived at *ABC* company my supervisor was fired. Then our group had five different managers within a year and you became our sixth. While this was going on, my budget was dissolved and I had to raise it again by creating programs for every agency. This enabled me to launch the first national direct-marketing campaign this company has ever had. Ted, I did my job. Do you really think two weeks is fair?

Ted: Well . . . no.

Me: What do you think is fair?

Ted: Three months?

Me: Thanks, Ted. But how is this payable?

Ted: It's all in the papers. Here, we'll pay it out as salary over the three months.

Me: But what if I get another job before the time is up?

Ted: That wouldn't matter at all, we would owe you the severance. You could get another job tomorrow and we would still owe you the severance.

Me: Well that's a good policy, but I need a lump sum.

Ted: Really? Well I'm sure I could arrange that but it may mean that your benefit period is shortened; you should ask about that.

Me: That's OK. So how are you going to announce my departure?

Ted: I thought I'd send out a memo saying that your position was eliminated and that you were pursuing other options.

Me: You know, Ted, if you give me till Monday you could send out a much better memo.

Ted: Why, do you have another offer?

Me: Yes I do but I'm still negotiating it, and I need till Monday.

Ted: OK, you've got it, but I can't wait after that.

Me: That won't be a problem.

Ted: It's probably not the best for you to be hanging out here until Monday. How are we going to explain why you're not here this week?

Me: I wasn't planning to be here; I'm the keynote speaker at the *xyz* international marketing conference on Friday.

Ted: Wow, that's great. I had no idea.

Me: Thanks. So let's go down to human resources together to work out any kinks in that lump sum.

Ted: OK sounds good; let's go.

While I was a keynote speaker at the prestigious international marketing conference, I was negotiating the other offer long distance. It just so happened that I had been nursing this external offer along for a rainy day. It was a great job and they came through with a $20,000 increase in salary while I was at the conference. I accepted the offer and returned to firm *ABC* to collect my belongings. Ted dropped by and said, "I redid the memo and wanted to run it by you." I approved of his new memo. Then Ted said a surprising thing: "Now you should write me a resignation letter for the files." I was incredulous and reminded him that he had laid me off—*he had forgotten!*

Resignation Payments and Exit Bonuses for Salespeople

Why don't star performers who resign get severance? They don't get it if they don't ask for it. If you want it, here's a way to get it. Go to the person who has the authority and budget to pay the severance and ask for it. Follow up in writing immediately. I had the same basic conversation after leaving two different sales jobs and got payments in the $5K range in both cases (far less than what I requested but still something). In both cases my bosses became my advocate and asked their bosses for a severance payment for me. Both of them felt that I should be paid commissions on my sales that would be paid by clients after my departure. Here's how my conversation went when I left these companies:

Dialogue #5

Me: Thanks for taking a few minutes to touch base with me today.

Mary: What's on your mind?

Me: I'd like you to support me in my decision to leave *ABC* company.

Mary: You've got to be kidding. You're leaving? Your team just made $6 million in sales in the last quarter. I can't believe this. I thought you were having a great time!

Me: Yes, we did do well. Mary, you know we worked very hard for these sales. I believe a fair severance is three months' commissions and salary because I earned this.

Mary: You are serious. So where are you going?

Me: I've accepted a position as the x at company y. They are not a client yet but they have a good potential of becoming a substantial one.

Mary: Well, I'm sure we could provide just that same kind of opportunity here.

Me: Mary, company y offers me the opportunity to learn more about a, b, and c. That doesn't exist here. I need this experience for my future. But in the next two weeks I will deliver that special assignment you requested. Mary, you have the authority to support me in this decision. I have done well for this company. Do you think three months' severance is fair?

Mary: . . . err . . . I need to think about it.

Me: Well, here is my written notice of my intention to resign two weeks from today. I guess I'll leave the three months' severance request in the note, but it would probably be cleaner if we could agree upon the severance issue today. What do you think is fair?

Mary: I really can't say, I need to check with human resources on our policies.

Me: Thanks for your help, Mary. Will I hear from you today on this?

Mary: I'll get on it immediately.

Me: Thanks, Mary. I'll get that assignment to you pronto and I'm looking forward to working together in my new role.

Exit Bonus for a Salesperson

Some salespeople negotiate severance when they are taking a new job if they are required to execute a non-compete for the new job, because the non-compete limits the salesperson's income after leaving the firm. One person said, "I will agree that I'm not going to pursue any of the accounts you have me working on for *x* amount of time, but in turn I want some kind of guarantee that you're going to carry my income for a period after I leave, because otherwise I'm locked out of supporting myself."

Double-Whammy Opportunities: Simultaneous Bonuses

Have you figured out this happy topic? There's nothing wrong with reviewing the list below and memorizing the permutations of possibilities:

signing bonus + severance = double whammy

signing bonus + year-end bonus = double whammy

signing bonus + relocation allowance = double whammy

signing bonus + home buyout = double whammy

signing bonus + trailing spouse allowance = double whammy

As you know, these figures are additive, and life gets even more interesting *past* double whammies! Best of luck in figuring out your own combinations.

Summary

The trick with bonuses is to seize the moment. Many jobs have become risky—less secure and shorter in tenure. Risk costs money and it's part of your compensation. If you consider accepting a new job of undefined tenure, your signing bonus is some compensation for the risk.

Another approach is to add up all the bonuses ahead of time and contract a job for a defined time period at a higher price. This could take the form of a first-year guarantee or a fixed-length contract for a different time period. Depending on the demand for your skills, you may have the opportunity to earn far more in less time.

You may also be compensated for risk when you leave a job, especially during a restructuring. The person who terminates your employment may not even know you well and she is in an awkward situation. Be prepared for this cherished moment. Analyze your company's goals ahead of time. Visualize in detail exactly how you will capitalize on the opportunities. When you talk to the decision maker, be sure he is very familiar with your particular circumstance. For example, it's helpful to review that you were relocated, that your performance was fine, and that you would like to work together in the future. Ask him to be fair.

There is nothing to lose and quite a bit to gain!

Negotiating the Rest of Your Compensation

Tactics 28–35:

28. Create an offer checklist
29. Benefit from relocation payments
30. Company car
31. Company credit card
32. Employee at will with a first-year guarantee
33. Delay your acceptance to increase the offer (dialogue #1)
34. Divide and conquer your offer (dialogue #2)
35. Deal with the unoffer offer (dialogue #3)

Bonuses are flashy but the rest of your compensation also needs to be negotiated. I find that an offer checklist helps.

Create an Offer Checklist

After a company that you're interested in makes an initial offer, it is important to get clear in your mind all the different cash and non-cash components of the entire package. You may want to make an offer checklist for each job, in order to make sure you can get answers to all your important questions.

You should know the information at the top of the offer checklist before you start talking about compensation. Next, itemize the parts of the offer in order of importance. Do all the math ahead of time so that you have better information going into discussions.

Some jumpers avoid verifying their current salary. These candidates turn the question around and ask, "Well, what is the job worth?" Trying to get a range of what the job is worth can be a good idea if you have been recruited to a job way over your current salary. However, with a recruiter, this tactic of salary evasion generally does not work.

Before accepting an offer, you need to understand the organization and your role in it as well as the compensation package. The compensation package should include the benefit and relocation package, so be sure to get this information before finalizing the offer. Within the benefits look for 401K eligibility upon acceptance. Also note the percent pretax you can save and the percent that is matched by the company savings plan.

Benefit from Relocation Payments

Some jumpers have noted that their best opportunities come with relocations. In the words of one executive, "If they could not find anyone locally, and they want you badly enough that they're going to move you across the country, they're usually willing to pay pretty well to do that. Relos and signing bonuses go hand in hand." Also look for lovely little gifts like relocation

Sample Offer Checklist for a Vice President of Marketing Job

Present organization and my role:
- Structure of the current organization?
- Scope of the vice president of marketing position?
- Includes building customer database?
- Includes salespeople (to sell ads to strategic partners)?
- Staff upon acceptance of job?
- Current marketing budget?
- How is the marketing budget currently derived?
- Who funds the direct-marketing budget?
- Distribution of marketing budget by marketing channel?
- What are the steps to completing the sale?
- CEO's opinion of the direct-marketing group?

Future organization and my role:
- Structure of the future organization (SVPs instead of VPs)?
- Career path of VP, marketing?
- Growth of the marketing staff?

The compensation:
- Base?
- Bonuses?
- Stock options (including number of, price upon acceptance of job, and when they can be sold)?
- Commission on direct contracts sold?

- First-year guarantee amount?
- Relocation policy and gross up (taxes the company agrees to pay for you)?
- 401K or pension plan eligibility first year?
- Family health insurance?
- Current vacation time allowed (paid and unpaid)?

Other negotiating points:
- Title of job position?
- Office location on floor?
- Promotion of career change to employee's contacts and the press?
- Start date?
- Need a portable computer?
- Paid severance?
- Administrative assistant?

Future strategies:
- Golden parachute in case company is sold, taken over, fails, or is restructured?
- What happens if the legal entity changes?
- Annual base pay raises?
- Annual increase in bonus percentage?
- Annual stock options?
- Future vacation time allowed (paid and unpaid)?

Just wondering:
- Health club in building?
- Cafeteria in building?
- Where is staff located on floor?

allowance payments, trailing spouse payments, decorating allowances, and payments of real estate fees for purchasing or renting a house. If you think that you will get the job and take it, then look at properties before the offer is finalized. This gives you a better idea of the value of the full offer, including cost-of-living changes. It also helps you to understand what it would be like to live in this new place.

Company Car

Be sure to investigate the offer of a company car. There are some catches that you need to be aware of. If your name is on the lease and you leave the company, you may be stuck with a car and a lease. Some people prefer to buy their own car and be paid a constant amount each month for its use. There are many options to consider. It is best to check out the long-term financial consequences of the company's offer prior to accepting it.

Company Credit Card

Although the terms of a company credit card are generally not part of an employment negotiation, you may want to revisit your current company's policy before jumping. In some cases the employee is still responsible for the bill and it is up to the company to reimburse the employee. I have also heard of cases where the company pays the credit card directly and responsibility switches to the employee if the employee leaves the company. This can be a problem if you have company expenses on your card at the time that you leave the company. If you sign up for a company credit card, you need to know who is ultimately responsible for paying the bill.

Employee at Will with a First-Year Guarantee

Sometimes it can be more lucrative to create a closed-end agreement that can be renewed with both parties' consent. This enables you to guarantee your salary for a certain period, such as for the first year. You may want to include or exclude health benefits in your contract. Sometimes it works well to create an employee-at-will type of agreement with a first-year guarantee. This way you guarantee front-loaded payments but can still have the upside possibility of high payments in following years.

Delay Your Acceptance to Increase the Offer

Dialogue #1

I found out about this delay tactic by accident. I was doing my job and enjoying it but my company was undergoing slash-and-burn restructurings, which always had their ups and downs. One day I was talking with a vendor who was an old friend. He implored me to interview for a vacancy at his firm. So I figured what the heck, it's always good to have a spare job on call, I'll do the interview. This firm was extremely positive about me from the first interview. I didn't know how I felt about them because I didn't have time to think about it. They called me for a second interview and I did it. They were still very positive and I was still busy.

Then this potential employer wanted to fly in a psychologist to do a profile on me and needed an entire afternoon out of my life. I told them the only time that I had carved out to take off was the morning after a red-eye flight. They said they'd take me then. The plane had its usual tarmac delays so the all-nighter lasted through mid-morning. I drove from the airport to the meeting without a shower, in yesterday's clothes, and arrived late. I sank down into a large velvet armchair in a plushly carpeted, windowless, dimly lit room, and the doc softly asked questions about my first childhood memories. There were other arcane personal questions on topics I've never thought about and have since forgotten. When we got to timed written exercises on trains running in opposite directions, I told the guy I was skipping them. We had both known when arranging the meeting that I would not have slept much in the last twenty-four hours. I explained that under these circumstances my score would be enhanced by spending more time on the other parts instead.

A couple of weeks later, I figured what the heck, I'll finish this off. I sent the decision maker a Heinecke personalized card (see page 50). The card was quite flattering to the decision maker and extremely specialized. It featured a cartoon and a professionally written caption that was personalized with the decision maker's name. I also scheduled a meeting with him through his secretary for the day after he'd get the card. We met and he gave me a verbal offer. He loved the card! I responded in the meeting that the offer was really too low for me to consider. He asked me to think it over.

I then scheduled a meeting for two weeks into the future, with someone who would matrix manage me in the firm. After a week, I got a fairly anxious call from the decision maker: "Hey, how come I haven't heard from you?" I said, "I told you the offer was far too low for me to consider. I also need to talk to

Ms. *X* who would matrix manage me." He said, "Well we can't wait another week, we'll ask her to call you sooner."

Soon I got a call from the matrix manager. We had a good talk about the proposed job and I explained that the offer was $20K too low. She broke forces with the decision maker and became my internal advocate, sending him an e-mail, which was apparently pretty explicit. Very soon after, they called me with an offer that was $20K higher.

All this for a job I really wasn't thinking about pursuing. For me, it was a spare offer to contemplate on a rainy day. However, now it had become worth thinking about and I accepted it!

Divide and Conquer Your Offer

Dialogue #2

Just as in the previous example, the hiring "team" doesn't always act like a team. In another circumstance, one recruiter arranged an interview for me with company A, division 1. Another recruiter arranged an interview for me with the same company but in another division. Since human resources in division 1 *never* talked to human resources in division 2, I went along just fine on parallel tracks through two rounds of interviews with both divisions.

In the second round, I informed both decision makers of the situation. By their own arrangement (or disarrangement, if you please), I became more attractive to both decision makers because they actually had to come to terms with it. I'm convinced their mutual interest increased their mutual attraction to my candidacy. Consequently, they decided to cooperate with each other and provided a very competitive offer.

Deal with the Unoffer Offer

Dialogue #3

This one takes the cake! The recruiter told me that I was the front-runner of two finalists for a vice president of marketing position with an airline. I really wanted this job and had done an immense amount of research, including reading two books on the airline industry. I had worked out some innovative, dynamite marketing ideas and was eager to try them out.

All the interviewing for both candidates had been done and the decision maker was deliberating. The recruiter told me that they'd call with the answer Friday or Monday. He called on Monday and said, "We offered the job to the other candidate on Friday and we've been negotiating with her all weekend. We don't think she is going to take the job. We'd like to read you the offer we gave her and see if there is anything you object to in case you are offered this job."

In this situation, the recruiter is not presenting a situation that is advantageous to you. They have taken away your biggest bargaining chip, your confidence that the company wants you and you alone. If you comment negatively on the offer, you may be out of the running. If you say that the offer is fine, you have lost the opportunity to negotiate it up. The only way that I see to turn this situation around is to (1) wait until they decide that they want you and, (2) then negotiate it up.

This is how I replied: "OK, read me the offer." The recruiter read me an awful offer below my compensation range and with absolutely no vacation the first year. Then I said, "You know, it's really difficult to imagine how I would feel about the offer unless it was offered to me." The recruiter tried again a few times to get my comments and I said about the same thing back. A few days later the recruiter called to say that the other candidate had taken the job.

Win some, lose some. I needed to negotiate the terms in order for the job to be attractive to me. Yet I could only negotiate the terms if I knew that the employer wanted me and me alone.

P.S.: This same recruiter called back nine months later and asked if I'd like to sell jet engines!

Summary

The key to negotiating the rest of your compensation is preparation and practice (just like most things). It takes preparation to understand all the components of the offer. Then you need to get completely in touch with how you and your family feel about the offer. Practice all the scenarios of possible negotiation discussions. Visualize winning dialogues and they will spring forth at just the right moment.

A Painless Overview of Employment Contracts and Employment Law

Topics:
- The concept of at-will employment
- Which types of lawsuits have provided awards to employees?
- The role of the employee handbook
- The features of a good employment contract
- Freedom of speech on the job
- Finding an employment lawyer
- Checking your own references
- Sources of more information

F or most of us, employment contracts and employment law are not exactly scintillating subjects. But before your eyes glaze over, read this chapter—it's got information in it that you really need to know. Employment law has far-reaching consequences, not only for each of us personally, but for the entire future of work. We are going to breeze through this subject in an appealing way, by speaking with an expert who is fascinated by the field.

Steve Hyman is a partner in the law firm Leavy Rosensweig and Hyman, and is president of the New York Civil

Liberties Union. His firm specializes in employment law and is located in New York City.

Hartman: Steve, thank you for offering to speak to us. By way of introduction, could you tell us a bit about some of the prominent, successful cases that you've argued on behalf of employees?

Hyman: The specifics are confidential, but I can tell you about a couple of our cases that were publicized on Court TV and in other media. One was called *Cherry v. Coudert Brothers*, where an employee sued her employer. We settled the case on the evening before the jury was about to decide the case. The jury indicated that they would have found discrimination and the client wanted to settle. The amount of the settlement is confidential, but the client was satisfied.

Another publicized case is *Flynn v. Goldman Sachs*. It's one of the leading cases in the investment banking area. It posed a victory and a loss because we were able to convince a jury that Flynn was discriminated against even though Goldman Sachs used a woman to fire her, although the judge then reversed the verdict. This was a prominent case, which helped establish some law in the area.

People need to understand the nature of the victory when an employee sues an employer. Jury verdicts do happen but they have high costs and they don't always go your way.

Hartman: So settlements are generally a more successful approach?

Hyman: They certainly are something you aim for. A client should understand that.

The Concept of At-Will Employment

Hartman: Most of our readers are employed by private enterprise; they are not government employees. In this context, can you define, for our readers, *at-will employment?*

Hyman: At-will employment is a very straightforward concept. It means that you are hired by an employer and that you or the employer can terminate that arrangement at any time. That is the basic concept.

Hartman: Is this covered by state law?

Hyman: Yes, that is correct. It is a concept that we would call *rising out of the common law,* or legal system, but it is established in each state jurisdiction as a particular concept and there are varieties of at-will because that gets modified. It's up to each individual state. There's no federal common law concept of at-will.

Hartman: Illinois seems to be known as being a very pro-employer, at-will type of state. Are there are other states viewed as more pro-employee or less at-will? Can you tell us which states are like Illinois? Is there any way for someone moving into a new state to look this up?

Hyman: That would take research because you are dealing with fifty different jurisdictions. New York, for instance, is a very pro-employer state. It is stronger in some ways than in Illinois. New York has taken a very hard line that in order to have a contract, under New York law, you really have to have a specific agreement. Illinois has, in my view, a more liberal approach to its view of a contract than New York. Connecticut has an even more liberal view.

119

There are states that are not necessarily at-will; they have some requirement of cause. Even where there is a contract you can always be terminated for cause and then the question is what is cause, which is a legal definition. In most states the *cause* concept is something that would be discussed within the context of an agreement or an employee manual. It has to be a serious reason materially related to one's character or job performance. An example of a character problem would be a conviction for selling illegal drugs or stealing money from your employer.

Hartman: Is there a trend in employment law regarding at-will employment? In terms of laws being made over the years, are more states going toward at-will or are more states continuing to change it?

Hyman: Again, that would be something to research state by state. Some states are beginning to find ways to chip away at the concept of at-will. There are cases where certain acts of employers or manuals constitute a contract so that there is a concept of protection for the employee. Other states are moving in the direction of a much more protective environment for the employer.

Which Types of Lawsuits Have Provided Awards to Employees?

Hartman: Steve, could you provide an overview of which types of lawsuits seem to win for employees and why?

Hyman: In an employment at-will state, the only things that will win are those that are protected by statutes. For instance, discrimination, sexual harassment, fraud, contractual disputes, and public-policy issues, such as whistle-blowing. If you are a woman, if you are a minority, if you are over forty, if you are disabled, then you have certain rights that do not exist for those who are the majority, under forty, are male, and so on. Thus, if a reason for termination is based upon discrimination, you can sue and it is on this basis that employees have prevailed.

Sexual harassment is another area where it's possible to sue and win. Fraud is the luring of an employee into taking a job alleging that the job will either have longevity or that it will be a great opportunity and all of that is not true. This is where an employee is misled into believing that he or she has a job and does not—it's sometimes exacerbated by relocating the new employee. Another area that can succeed would be a situation in which you can prove that a contract, whether oral or written, was violated. People should know that oral contracts can be valid, but there has to be the establishment of a contract in some form. And finally you have the limited area of public policy, which can be used successfully. This includes public-policy rules such as the whistle-blower, or for instance, in Connecticut, violating an employee's First Amendment rights.

The Role of the Employee Handbook

Hartman: Let's explore the role of the employee handbook regarding employment law. Is there a relationship between the employee handbook and an employment contract? If you have both, which one takes precedence?

Hyman: The contract will always take precedence. The hand-book is not always considered the equivalent of a contract and employers often have disclaimers in them so that they cannot be relied upon in court. A contract is, in fact, binding on the part of the parties who have the power to agree. Either oral or written, it is a contract. So the contract will control.

Hartman: Most executives are given an employee handbook. Are there any sections we should read before accepting a job?

Hyman: The handbook is a two-edged sword; it both gives you rights and takes them away. It will, however, determine certain principal aspects of employment that you should look for. One is what kind of termination procedures are used. The second is what kind of severance it calls for. Almost every employer has had a lawyer review their handbook and the handbook will state that it is not a contract. That is done in order to keep the at-will employment concept alive and not undone. Some states have chipped away at that. New York started to do so but is now drawing back again from the concept that the manual will determine the terms of your employment. It may but it is still not a contract, which causes a great deal of confusion. Should you read it? Yes.

Hartman: Before taking a job?

Hyman: Yes. The only way that you can modify the implications of the manual is to have a written contract—and that depends on your bargaining position. For instance, some manuals say that you can't be fired except for cause—the procedure is to give warnings and treat employees fairly. The other side of the coin is that it is not a binding contract. The employer may not adhere to it and they may come in one day and say that you're fired. Does the manual control? If it is not a contract, but merely a guide, it doesn't control. So, I think that an employee should realize that the manual is only a guide. Without a written contract, it cannot necessarily protect them the way employees might think.

The Features of a Good Employment Contract

Hartman: It would be helpful to have a checklist of what should be included in an employment contract. This way you know what to talk about with your potential supervisor. When they give you a written offer, everything you discussed with them should be in it. Because your firm has created hundreds of employment contracts, can you review for us what the features are of a good employment contract?

Hyman: All of the following questions should be addressed:

- How long are you guaranteed employment?
- What is the nature is your compensation?
- What is the nature of your job?
- Under what terms can you be terminated?
- If terminated, what kind of severance do you get?
- Are there any restrictions on future employment?
- Are you bound to submit your claim to arbitration? (Arbitration is a common feature in the securities industry and becoming a more common feature in commercial America generally.)

Hartman: What is the range in salaries of executives who are using employment contracts?

Hyman: Well, that will vary. You have executives making hundreds of thousands of dollars. . . . I've seen contracts in the $50,000+ area; less than that and they're not useful. It really depends on your position with the company. If you're going to be working for a young start-up company, you can get a contract at a lower salary because there may not be a lot of employees. If you go to a major company, such as Pepsi or Mobil, you'll find that you are not going to get a contract unless you are a high-level executive earning hundreds of thousands of dollars.

Freedom of Speech on the Job

Hartman: Do private employees have freedom of speech?

Hyman: Generally, no. The concept of free speech is, under the Constitution, a concept that is between the individual and the government. So, "Congress shall make no law . . . abridging the freedom of speech" is a concept that applies only to a public employee who has a job with the government. For instance, a public employee says, "I don't like the Democrats," and gets fired. That is a violation of free speech. On the other hand, under the same circumstances in the private arena where there is at-will employment and no contract, an employee can say, "I don't like the Democrats," and the boss can say, "I don't want you working here anymore." Some states have passed laws that prohibit this in some limited way but it would take state-by-state research to identify them.

Finding an Employment Lawyer

Hartman: How do you find an employment lawyer?

Hyman: Some bar associations break down lawyers by specialty. Not in New York, for instance, but in some jurisdictions. Some organizations dedicated to employment law, such as the National Employment Lawyers Association, would be able to provide you with names. Probably as good a way as any is the same way you find a specialist in medicine—you use your family doctor. In this case, use your family lawyer. Lawyers generally know other lawyers who specialize in the area. If you do seek a lawyer, they have an ethical and professional obligation to keep your case confidential, regardless of whether you select that particular lawyer to represent you.

Hartman: Steve, thank you for your comments.

Checking Your Own References

Now that you've gotten a taste of employment law, here is the way to review what your employers are saying about you. Contact a company such as Documented Reference Check, which contracts with agencies to contact your past employers for a reference on you. They then provide you with a written transcript of what your employers said. For more information on this firm read the *Wall Street Journal* article dated November 11, 1996, page B1, or contact them at:

Documented Reference Check
1174 Diamond Bar Blvd., #243

Diamond Bar, CA 91765
Order Desk: 800-742-3316
Direct Line: 909-629-0317

Sources of More Information

Internet

Martindale, Hubble offers a lawyer locator service.
Search by the specialty labor and employment:
http://lawyers.martindale.com/marhub

The Nolo website has additional help on legal issues with
a focus on helping yourself: http://www.nolo.com

Association

National Employment Lawyers Association

Books

*Every Employee's Guide to the Law: Everything You Need to
    Know About Your Rights in the Workplace—And What to
    Do If They Are Violated* by Lewin G. Joel III, Pantheon
    Books, New York, 1993.

*Your Rights in the Workplace: An Employee's Guide to Legal
    Protection* by Richard L. Strohn, Career Press,
    Hawthorne, NJ, 1994.

Part Two

Jumpers at Home

Building Personal Wealth: Financial Tactics for Jumpers

Tactics 36–44:

36. Save early and often
37. Use IRAs, Keoghs, and 401K plans to maximize savings and investment
38. Minimize taxes
39. Buying versus renting homes: It's not what you have, it's what you do
40. Life insurance: Eliminate worry about your dependents
41. Health insurance: Buy it as an independent
42. About unemployment insurance
43. Keep your credit report pristine
44. Take advantage of portable payment vehicles

Over the years, I've enjoyed all of my various jobs. Lots of these assignments required changing companies and relocating. If you jump often, you create a unique lifestyle. The choices that my family and I have made regarding personal financial services have supported, even fueled, our mobile lifestyle. Jumpers must figure out a way to make their personal finances portable, convenient, and worry free.

This chapter is not meant to be an overview of personal financial services. Instead, the information below is intended to illustrate how certain financial services can support your jumping lifestyle. If you've already got at least one year's salary saved and you're a prudent and savvy investor, you may just want to skip to particular areas where you have questions, such as the issue of buying or renting a house (page 140) or purchasing health insurance (page 145).

Save Early and Often

Saving money is an important strategic move. It's important to build up a nest egg quickly, as soon as you start working. As quickly as possible, you should save enough so that you can survive without your regular salary for at least one year. Obviously, the more the better. This will give you freedom and peace of mind.

Think of these savings as seed money for "You, Inc." You will be surprised at how much more independent and risk-taking you'll be with your career if you know that the world will not end if you decide to leave a job or if you get fired.

The ability to jump is a good reason *not* to live at the top level of your income. If you have no cushion, you may need to stay in a job just because you need the money. That's no way to live: Remember, it's not what you have, it's what you do. Go out a little less, stay away from the fancy restaurants, forgo long, fancy vacations, and bank it.

A rule of thumb is that it takes an average of a month for every $10,000 of salary to find another job. In other words, a $60,000-a-year job may take six months to find—plan accordingly. Your quality of life will be amazingly enhanced by having a year or two of salary in the bank.

To maximize savings, lets talk a bit about investing. Which savings plan would provide the most money after fifteen years: (1) saving $500 a month at a 5 percent annual return or (2) saving $400 a month at 9 percent? You end up with more money in option two. Option one yields $133,644 and option two yields $151,362. In option two you deposited $18,000 less but you saved $17,718 more because your money earned a higher rate of interest. The *rate of return* on your savings is just as important as the amount you save. Consequently we'll review the different options you have when saving money.

When you examine various investment options, you will run across some common terms. One refers to *rate of return* (or *nominal rate of return*), which means the percent return that your investment is getting. If you deposit $100 into a savings account and, after one year, have $105, your rate of return is 5 percent. Sometimes you see *annualized* rate of return. You will be promised 12 percent annualized for two months. To go back to our original example, a deposit of $100 will net you $2 after two months, but then the rate will drop to whatever the constant rate is. Another important term is *real* rate of return (also known as *inflation adjusted*), which means that the inflation rate has been subtracted from the return. If a money market account is paying 5 percent and the inflation rate is 3 percent, your real rate of return is 2 percent. This measurement, the real rate of return, is usually used when comparing different types of investments.

The main types of investments are money markets, stocks, bonds, and real estate. Over time, average rates of return on these investments have been observed (real estate is a different, complex animal and will be dealt with later in this chapter). In nominal terms, money markets return, at the present time, (approximately) 4 percent, bonds return 6 percent, and stocks return 12 percent. In nominal terms, stocks return three times what bonds return.

Now let's look at real rates of return. Using 2 percent as the inflation factor, money market accounts return approximately 2 percent percent, bonds return 4 percent, stocks return 10 percent. In real terms, therefore, stocks look spectacular!! Their return is five times that of money markets and two and a half times that of bonds.

What are these varying rates of return telling you? Let's look at risk. In all investing, the most important rule to remember is that the higher the return, the higher the risk. The market will always tell you how risky any investment is. Just find out what the risk-free (money market) rate is, and compare the prospective investment to that rate. The reason the real rate of return on stocks is five times greater than the return on money markets is that the market considers stocks to be five times as risky. The next time that a broker wants to sell you a "safe" bond that yields 11 percent, when every other safe bond you know is yielding 6 percent, remember: It isn't safe. If it was, it would be yielding what all the other safe bonds yield.

Essentially, once you know the respective rates of return on the different classes of investments (money markets, bonds, and stocks) and their respective risks, you are ready to allocate your assets among these different classes of investments. *Asset allocation* depends entirely on your tolerance for risk—it's also known as "not putting all your eggs in one basket." If it makes you nervous to see the value of your investments plummet by 10 percent in a week, perhaps you should not be in the stock market. You might find its volatility an extremely unpleasant experience. On the other hand, your investment time horizon comes into play here. The longer your time horizon is, the less concerned you need to be with the volatility of any investment.

Actually, the longer your time horizon is, the less volatility there is. The stock market only jumps around like crazy when you look at it week to week. If you compared several different five-year periods, you would find that the stock market was not jumping around that much.

For example, take the years 1950 to 1980. According to *Investment Policy* by Charles Ellis (Irwin Professional Publications, 1993), in the worst *year* the stock market lost about 26 percent of its value. In the worst five-year period, it lost about 12.5 percent of its value. During the worst fifteen-year period, however, it gained 4.3 percent on average for each year. For the worst twenty-five-year period, it gained, on average, 8.4 percent per year. As you can see, if you left your money in the market for at least fifteen years during this period, you would have had a positive return. During this thirty-year period, the average annual rate of return on stock investments was 10 percent. It has since increased to over 12 percent.

Armed with this knowledge, and knowing that your investment time horizon is twenty-five years or more, a disciplined investor might well choose to put the majority of her investments into the stock market. I am a cautious investor. I currently have a twenty-five-year time horizon for my investments. I have invested 15 percent in cash, 12 percent in bonds, 8 percent in international stocks, and the balance, 65 percent, in the U.S. stock market in a reputable mutual fund, the Vanguard Group's Index 500 fund.

This mutual fund and other index funds like it simply mimic the performance of the S&P 500. You can't beat the market with this fund; it *is* the market. And it consistently beats 90 percent of the other mutual funds around.

Use IRAs, Keoghs, and 401K Plans
to Maximize Savings and Investment

In case this has not been emphasized enough, please understand that jumping is very risky, very difficult, and not for the fainthearted. It strengthens your ability to pursue the career of your dreams if you plan for a period of unemployment as a safety net. Consequently, you need to be an aggressive saver whenever possible.

IRAs, Keoghs, and other tax-advantaged savings plans are great. They are so good, in fact, that it sometimes pays to borrow the money to fund them. For example, if April 15 rolls around and you just don't have the cash to put $2,000 into your IRA, it would be a smart financial strategy to borrow the money, assuming you could pay it off within a year or so at the right interest rate. If you are in the 30 percent tax bracket, making the $2,000 deposit would save you $600 in the current tax year. If you borrowed the $2,000 at 15 percent, and were able to pay it off in one year, your interest expense would be $300. Obviously, if you borrowed the money at 19 percent and couldn't pay it off for three years, you shouldn't do it. You must determine whether your interest payments over the life of the loan would be less than the $600 you would save. But remember, you will be getting back an extra $600 if you make the deposit (assuming you are due a refund), so that leaves only $1,400 to pay back. If you have a tax liability, it will be $600 less if you make the contribution. You are going to have to come up with an extra $600 to pay the IRS, so why not come up with $2,000 and pay yourself?

Another great deal are 401Ks. For maximum savings, always take the maximum that you can out of every paycheck.

Because of the tax deduction, it's like getting (the first year), a return equal to your tax deduction. If you are in the 30 percent bracket, that's a 30 percent return. Beg or borrow (but don't steal) to take advantage of these deductions.

Many people think that once you make an IRA or Keogh deposit the money can't be touched until you retire. This is not true. There are penalties, but depending on your situation and your need for the money, the penalties are not onerous. If you take an IRA distribution before retirement, the distributor may withhold 10 percent and send it to the IRS where it will be added to your regular withholding for the year. It is still your money. When you do your taxes in April of the following year, if you are due a refund, the money that was withheld from your IRA distribution also is available to be refunded to you. It is just like withholding on your salary. If you have a low income that year you will be able to get most of it back in the form of a refund. There is also an additional 10 percent penalty on any premature IRA distribution, payable at tax time.

Let's look at what is really happening. When things are going well and you're making good money, you are depositing money into your IRA or Keogh. Let's say you are in the 30 percent marginal tax bracket. This means that you don't have to pay taxes on 30 percent of whatever you deposit. For example, you deposited $2,000 in 1994 and saved $600 in taxes. Now, say you have been laid off. After a few months, you start dipping into your IRA. Your income will be much lower, and your marginal tax rate will probably be closer to 15 percent.

Let's say that you pull out $2,000 from your IRA in 1995. You have two liabilities with respect to this money. At the end of 1995, you do your taxes and you are in the 15 percent bracket, so your income taxes on the $2,000 are $300 ($2000 ×

15 percent = $300). The 10 percent penalty equals $200 ($2,000 × 10 percent = $200). You saved $600 in taxes in 1994, and you had to pay only $500 in taxes in 1995 when you took an early distribution, so your cash flow profit is $100. There's no magic in this. It happens because, as your income goes up, your marginal tax rate goes up. When you have a good income and are in the 25 percent or 30 percent bracket, tax benefits are very valuable. Conversely, if your income drops, your tax rate drops, and tax benefits or penalties are not as valuable or costly.

To support your jumping lifestyle, push to make the maximum deposit you can into every tax-advantaged vehicle open to you. If things turn out less than rosy, you can get your money out and you will usually be better off than if you had never made the deposit.

Minimize Taxes

As you saw in the examples above, unless you can judge the tax consequences of your savings and income-generating activities, it is difficult to maximize your savings. The best way to understand the tax consequences is to do your own taxes. The first year will be difficult, but after that it gets progressively easier. If you absolutely cannot deal with this, you should hire someone, not to do your taxes for you, but to *help you do them*. The reason I stress this is because if you don't know the nuts-and-bolts details of your return, the tax implications are very difficult to assess and it is consequently more difficult to maximize your savings.

If you get a professional to help you the first year, and understand everything in your return, the next year will not be difficult. Even if your situation and job have changed, you will know how to fill in the blanks the next year. Although there are a thousand things to learn in the tax code, *you* don't need to learn all of them. You probably need to be an expert in about five things. As time goes by and you make more money every year, you can learn about one or two things each year.

For example, if you're a homeowner with a little consulting business, you must become familiar with Schedule A (on which you deduct your mortgage interest payments) and Schedule C (on which you list your income and expenses for your business), and perhaps you may need to learn Form 4562 (which covers depreciation of any equipment you've bought during the year). Every year, the same forms will be filled out exactly the same way; only the numbers change. If you get into buying and selling stock, you can learn about Schedule D and the wonders of capital gains. It's complicated, but like anything else in life, if you do it a little bit at a time it is not overwhelming. It's only once every year.

There are some great books out there to help you through the annual tax hassle. One of my favorites is John Reed's (no relation to the Citibank CEO) *Aggressive Tax Avoidance for Real Estate Investors* (Reed Publishing, 1987). Even if you're not a real estate investor, the first section, "The Aggressive Philosophy," should be required reading for every taxpayer. The other classics are those big yellow books you always see around tax time: *Guide to Income Tax* is published by Consumer Reports; another is by J. K. Lasser. Don't be intimidated by the size of these books; you will probably only be using about 25 pages. The rest of the things just won't apply to you.

Buying Versus Renting Homes:
It's Not What You Have, It's What You Do

Like many young couples, our first purchase was our dream house. My husband and I bought an ultramodern co-op loft in the middle of Manhattan. Unfortunately, we bought it in September of 1987, one month before the stock market crash. Two years later Citibank took it off our hands in a corporate relocation and lost $60,000 when they sold it—$60,000 in after-tax money in two years! Not many budgets can survive that hit. Think of how many years it would take to save $60,000.

After this shocking experience, my husband and I wear our MBA hats at home. We consider every real estate purchase as two things above all: (1) a highly leveraged, illiquid investment, and (2) an investment whose performance depends on factors almost totally outside of our control.

It sounds pretty risky, doesn't it? Do you want to make such an investment? Under certain circumstances it is great, and we have bought real estate again, many times. Because we have faced this question with every move, we've developed a realistic way to look at the rent versus buy decision.

These are our assumptions going in:

■ What you do is more important than what you have. Remember this advice from the Jumper Credo in Chapter Three? We decide to live somewhere because there is something of interest for us to do there. We do not know how long this period will last. We don't want to be trapped into staying somewhere because we own a house that we cannot sell or rent; we won't allow a single piece of real estate to require us to be anywhere in particular.

■ Money invested in real estate should earn a rate of interest that compensates us for risk.

■ Monthly payments in rent or mortgage cannot exceed one-quarter of our monthly pay.

Buying Investment Properties

That said, real estate can be part of your retirement and savings strategies. Put any properties that you purchase as a primary residence through the same review as investment properties—they should be looked at as investment properties first and foremost.

The Property Should Be Easy to Rent and Maintain

My husband and I only buy properties that we will sell when we need the money; hopefully that will be when we retire. If we do decide to live in a property, we do not know how long we will be living there and thus we assume it needs to be easily rented out and maintained after we leave. Focus your real estate investments in the types of properties that can be managed long distance, are easy to rent, have no outdoor maintenance, and have built-in support systems such as a superintendent or rental office. Properties in residential resort communities and apartments in major cities generally meet these criteria. Although this is the subject of other books, I predict that properties in residential resort communities will continue to appreciate faster than other residential properties because they (1) are much more limited in supply, and (2) they are better at meeting the needs of two-career families and retirees.

In order to make sure that the property will be easy to rent, place an ad in the local paper describing it as a rental, *before you buy the property.* Advertise it for the amount needed to cover the mortgage and the maintenance. For a property to be considered a good investment, you should get at least a dozen calls from individuals, not real estate agents, within two weeks of placing the ad. You can set up a temporary phone number in the local city using a voicemail service such as American Voicemail (cost is about $25.00).

The One-Quarter of Your Income Rule

The down payment should not be too much of a stretch. It should not take much more than half of your savings. If you are also living in the property, the monthly mortgage and maintenance payments should be within one-quarter of your monthly income. If you are not living in the property, the annual net income must produce over a 15 percent annual return on your investment of funds.

The Property Should Maintain Its Value

You should be convinced that the value of the property will not go down within the next ten years. Gain confidence in this by (1) reviewing the employer base of the community and (2) tracking the past sales of the property you are considering and several comparable properties. There should be a variety of industries represented by the employer base. For example, in Connecticut we found insurance and defense to be the primary industries and that most employers in both industries were downsizing; we didn't buy. In Illinois, however, we found a great variety of industries represented and we bought.

Find past sales information from the local assessor's office or tax office. Go look at the houses and find several that are comparable to yours. Look at sales within the last five years and then look at sales of these homes for the last fifteen years. The best information is if the same house has sold twice within the last five years.

Speak with the town assessor or appraiser. They are invaluable sources of information and most love to share their expertise. The same thing is true of real estate brokers, especially ones who have been in the business for a long time. For example, in Illinois we tracked a group of properties for fifteen years and the trend of the sale prices showed slow appreciation. In Connecticut, we saw the opposite trend. Both of these factors contributed to our decision to buy in Illinois and rent in Connecticut. We also saw that in Connecticut, the monthly payments to rent a house were far less than the monthly costs if we purchased the same house. That is a very important indicator. I would not recommend buying a house where the ownership costs are over 20 percent higher than the rental costs of the same house.

Renting Your Primary Residence

If the criteria for buying cannot be met, rent your primary residence and save your capital to buy other investment properties. When renting, the following criteria should be met:

- The lease needs to be at or below market level so that the house can be sublet in case you decide to leave.

- The rental payments need to be within one-quarter of your monthly income.

My family and I discovered some psychological advantages to renting. There's no large down payment—you stay liquid with a good-size amount of cash (or other investments) in the bank. There's no anxiety about whether this "investment" is going to bust your budget. You don't have ongoing concerns about maintenance and repair and you have no worries about whether or not you can sell if you have to.

Life Insurance: Eliminate Worry About Your Dependents

Term life insurance was definitely the best choice for my family. The tax advantages and investment opportunities of universal and whole life insurance were not as competitive as other financial vehicles. If you work for a large corporation, you can usually get term life insurance through your employer, but for jumpers there's a catch. The policies offered to employees are usually not portable. If you want uninterrupted coverage at a great value, you may need to buy it yourself.

Try researching it through the Internet. You can get most of your questions answered by searching under *insurance.* Several companies sell direct, allowing you to compare how much insurance you can get for the same cost. Be sure to compare the financial ratings of the companies.

Worksheets are available on the Internet to help you figure out how much insurance you need. Start by figuring out the amount of money your family would need each year if you weren't around. Subtract from this total the amount of income that would be generated by your savings and investments. The amount that would still be needed should then be divided by a reasonable rate of interest, say the rate on the thirty-year treasury bond. Suppose the shortfall was $25,000 per year and the current rate on the thirty-year bond was 6.5 percent. Dividing $25,000 by 6.5 percent would give you

$384,615. Therefore, it would be appropriate to purchase a $400,000 policy, which, when invested at 6.5 percent, would generate about $25,000 per year.

The second issue to consider when purchasing life insurance is what length of time the insurance should run. Consider the ages of your children and the length of time you need to keep paying the mortgage if you own your home. For example, if your child is ten years old and you have fifteen years left on your mortgage, fifteen years is a reasonable amount of time to have life insurance. In fifteen years your child will be twenty-five years old and contributing something to support himself, and your mortgage will be paid back. After fifteen years in this particular situation, life insurance is less crucial.

Health Insurance: Buy It As an Independent

This topic is relevant to jumpers who are between jumps (unemployed) or self-employed. If you formerly obtained health insurance through your employer, you can keep it under the regulations of COBRA (the Consolidated Omnibus Budget Reconciliation Act of 1986) after you leave. The problem is that without the subsidy from your employer, health insurance can be extremely costly. For example, if my family had taken COBRA, our insurance would have gone from $200 to $750 a month.

Although things are evolving quickly on the health-care front, two alternatives to COBRA that are currently available are worth mentioning: Golden Rule Insurance Company and insurance through the National Association for the Self-Employed (NASE). Both of these plans are particularly suited to healthy families or singles. Golden Rule offers several plan designs with benefits and premiums varying widely.

Golden Rule (which can be reached at 800-444-8990) also has an MSA option for self-employed individuals and their families. MSAs (Medical Savings Accounts) are a completely new product that was not available before January 1, 1997.

The Golden Rule MSA consists of two parts. The first part is a comprehensive major medical health plan. The plan pays for prescription drugs, doctor visits, surgery, hospital confinements, x-rays, lab work done in or out of the hospital, and preventative care up to $150 per covered individual. It does *not* pay for dental or vision expenses or deductibles. This means there is the possibility of significant out-of-pocket medical expenses during the year. That is where the second (MSA) part comes in. The MSA is like an IRA account from which you can withdraw money for these medical expenses.

All of the money that you put into an MSA is 100 percent deductible from your gross income. Again, think of it as an IRA account. In IRA accounts, you may put in up to $2,000 per year pre-tax. Pre-tax means exactly the same thing as being 100 percent deductible from gross income, that is, it reduces your income by that amount. In the case of an MSA, your annual deposit into the account is limited to 75 percent of your family deductible. (For a single, the percentage is a bit less.)

For example, my family consists of a husband in his early forties, a wife in her thirties, and a seven-year-old child. If we choose a $4,500 deductible, our payment for the medical insurance would be approximately $165 per month. In addition to this payment, we can deposit 75 percent of the deductible, or $3,375, into our MSA as a savings vehicle. If we are in the 30 percent tax bracket, that deposit of $3,375 will save us

$1,012 at tax time. We can then (unlike an IRA, which can only be distributed penalty-free after age 67) withdraw money from our MSA to pay uncovered medical expenses. We can spend the $3,375 for routine doctor visits, glasses, dental expenses, maternity expenses, and so on. Any amount we don't spend gets rolled over to the next year. Our total after-tax monthly expense, assuming we spend the entire $3,375 every year, comes out to $362 per month ($3,375, the original MSA deposit, less the tax deduction of $1,012 = $2,363. $2,363 divided into twelve monthly payments = $197 per month—add $197 to the $165 monthly premium to get $362). We get major medical coverage, plus $3,375 to spend on any medical expenses. Any money that we save gets rolled over. When we're over age sixty-five, we can withdraw money from the account with no penalty, but we must pay any income tax due, just as with an IRA distribution after age sixty-seven. Golden Rule's MSA currently credits 5 percent interest with no minimum balance.

A second alternative is an organization called the National Association for the Self-Employed, which endorses health insurance plans offered by different insurance companies. (NASE can be reached at 800-232-6273.) Members can apply for health-insurance plans from these insurers available at group rates. You can become a NASE member if you are self-employed or have an interest in being self-employed. The plans available through NASE cover only major medical emergencies, not routine and preventative care. Routine and preventative care costs would be paid directly by you and not reimbursed by the insurance company.

We purchased a policy for myself, my husband, and our seven-year-old son for approximately $350 per month, which includes maternity benefits. Without maternity benefits it would be about $250 per month. These insurance companies also offer an MSA option.

About Unemployment Insurance

If you are laid off, keep in mind that all the time that you were employed, your employer was paying for unemployment insurance. Employers pay quarterly taxes in order to fund this insurance program, which entitles you to weekly payments during the time that you are unemployed. Currently, the maximum benefit is approximately $330 per week. You can receive payments up to a maximum of approximately six months. I say approximately because these are state-run programs and each state has its own rules and regulations.

Be sure to file as soon as you are laid off (you do not qualify if you resign). Most states have a waiting period before benefits kick in, which can be as little as three days and as much as two or more weeks. During this period you are not entitled to benefits. The waiting period begins *after you file,* not when you are laid off. In other words, if you wait for three weeks after you are laid off to file for unemployment and your waiting period is two weeks, you are not entitled to benefits until five weeks have passed. Do not be afraid to use unemployment insurance and do not wait to file until you get behind in your rent before you apply.

There is also a possibility that you may be denied benefits. Your employer can contest your application. However, *Every Employee's Guide to the Law* by Lewin G. Joel III states that 90 percent of people who are fired or laid off get benefits and "one third of claimants who voluntarily quit [normally consid-

ered a disqualifying circumstance] are also awarded benefits"
(Pantheon Books, 1993, p. 262).

Another way to stretch your finances during periods of
unemployment is to immediately apply for deferments for all
loans that allow them. Student loans in particular have gener-
ous deferment programs. The Guaranteed Student Loan Program, depending on your particular loan program, sometimes
picks up the tab for accrued interest during the deferment
period. In other words, if you owe $15,000 on January 1 and are
in deferment until May 31, during those five months the federal
government pays the interest on your loan. On June 1, however,
you will still owe $15,000.

Keep Your Credit Report Pristine

Many people do not realize how critical their credit reports are
to their financial stability. The ability to access credit is essential
and to a large extent depends almost entirely on your credit
report. The first step is to immediately get copies of your credit
report from the three largest agencies: Experian (formerly
TRW), Trans Union, and Equifax. Experian will give you one
free copy per year. The others will charge about $10 for a copy
of your report. If you are turned down for credit, the bureau
that supplied the information to the prospective credit grantor
must send you a report for free.

Familiarize yourself with the codes that the reports use to
grade each account and check the entire report for errors. Send
the corrected version back using certified mail, so that you have
proof that you have disputed or corrected certain items.

Next, examine your credit report as if you were about to lend money to this person. Do the reports show consistent late payments?

Frequently, people send in mortgage, credit card, or student loan payments a few days late. This can occur because you are living paycheck to paycheck and are always a little short or may just be due to simple disorganization. If you have a lot of monthly bills, perhaps you've been finding it easier to pay them all at the end of the month. If all your bills are due the first of the month, this is fine. But if they're not (some student loan payments are due on the fifteenth of each month) you will be noted on the credit report as a chronic late payer, which can impede your ability to get future credit. Even worse, if you do manage to get credit, it may be at a significantly higher rate. If you have enough money to pay your bills, it is best to pay them on time. Nothing warms a banker's heart more than a perfect credit report. And don't forget that landlords routinely pull credit reports, as do some prospective employers.

Organize your bills and mail in each payment at least seven days before the due date. This gives you some insurance against the vagaries of the postal system. Also, be sure to watch the availability of funds in your account. Just because you have deposited a check into your account does not mean that the funds are available immediately. In some money market accounts, it takes as long as ten business days for the money to become available, which can mean a maximum of eighteen days before the money is available. For example, if you deposit a check on Friday, that day doesn't count. The business-day count begins the following Monday. The ten business days end with the close of business on Friday, two weeks after the deposit, but the money isn't available until the following Monday morning. If you count the first Friday as day one, the Monday that the money becomes available is day eighteen. Allow ample time for your deposits to clear.

When do you need credit? The most typical time is when you apply for a mortgage to buy a house. The cleaner your credit report is, the easier it will be to get a mortgage and the lower your interest rate will be. A tip about mortgages: If you have been turned down for a mortgage due to less than perfect credit, don't despair. Check with a good, experienced mortgage broker. These professionals usually work with dozens of lending institutions and will know which ones demand perfect credit records (A+) and which ones lend to people with A-, B, or even C credit.

Many people assume that if they don't owe any money they have excellent credit. Nothing could be further from the truth. The only way to build good credit is to borrow money, then pay it back according to the terms of the loan. If you own a house and have a mortgage, you're probably fine. But if you're just starting out, consider applying for credit cards or a small personal loan to start building up your credit. The longer your credit history, the better—it shows more experience at handling credit. It's one of those counterintuitive things, but the easiest time to get credit is when you don't need it. If you need it, you probably won't be able to get it.

When should you apply for credit? Aside from the mortgage scenario above, don't wait until you need credit to apply for it. Sometimes it is difficult to tell several months in advance whether you may want to leave a job or if you may soon get laid off. When you are happily employed, consider preparing for the worst and build up your credit options, because after you leave your job, you will not qualify for most loans or credit cards. You could take out a home equity loan or refinance your house and pull out some money. If you don't own a home, apply for some low-interest-rate credit cards. If it takes you a little longer than expected to find your next dream job, you will have the financial resources to enable you to keep looking until you do. By planning ahead, you are not forced to settle for an unsatisfactory job because you're running out of money.

Take Advantage of Portable Payment Vehicles

One of the most convenient ways to pay bills, especially if you frequently move, is by using an automatic bill payment system such as Citibank's Direct Access. The service is free and it is extremely easy to set up all your payments using your personal computer. They can be recurring payments, such as mortgage or rent payments, which go out on the same day and in the same amount every month. Or you can set up payees such as your phone or utility company and go online each month to pay bills for which the amount varies. By paying your bills using an automatic payment system, you're saving on postage and eliminating the hassle of writing checks.

For spending money, as opposed to paying bills, I highly recommend using a credit card for all your purchases and paying your bill in full every month. This means charging everything that you possibly can, including groceries, dry cleaning, gasoline, and any other small or large purchases for which the vendor will accept a credit card.

You can be compensated for using your credit card with frequent flyer miles, cash rebates, and a month's worth of float on your money. American Airlines and United Airlines have programs that give you one frequent flyer mile for every dollar that you spend. If you make sure to pay for everything with your card (rent! funerals! your car! use your imagination!), you can easily use it for a significant percentage of your total spending. At the current frequent flyer reward levels, if you spend $4,167 per month, in a year's time, you will have earned two round trip tickets to anywhere in the United States.

Other credit cards give you cash rebates at the end of the year. For example, if you spend $10,000 annually using the GE Rewards program, they will give you almost 2 percent cash back at the end of the year.

Credit cards are also helpful in budgeting. At the end of the year many credit cards will give you an annual statement that breaks down your spending by category. At the end of each month you get a statement that shows you how much you've spent and a detailed list, by category, of every single transaction you've spent your money on.

I've never been able to keep to a budget that said $400 for food this month, $75 for dry cleaning, $100 for restaurants, and so on. Too much paperwork, too much to keep track of! Too boring, too complicated! But if you pay for everything with your credit card, at the end of the month you will get a bill with a very definite number. If you want to budget, just bring that number down. If you want, you can even call the 800 number once a week to keep track of your spending.

Credit cards are also convenient to use. Cash is a pain to obtain and inconvenient to carry. You never know how much you have or whether it will be enough. Checks are a pain to carry and are environmentally and digitally incorrect. According to Martin Mayer, an international banking expert and the author of *The Banker: The Next Generation* (E.P. Dutton, 1997), the only reason that checks survive is because the Federal Reserve Bank makes a fortune processing them. Mayer believes that they have deliberately frustrated the growth of electronic commerce in this country because of that. So don't play into their hands!

Conclusion

Let's end the chapter by talking about saving again. Warren Buffet, the second richest man in America after Bill Gates, has said that before he buys anything, he thinks about the true value of the money he is spending. For example, if you're thinking about spending $500 on an expensive watch, remember: It's really costing you $2,330. That's what the $500 would have been worth had you invested it and gotten a return of 8 percent for twenty years.

Remember, money in the bank gives you freedom, because you owe yourself the right to walk. It makes you powerful, because you're ready to take the plunge when an irresistible opportunity presents itself. Suppose a great start-up company offers you a position paying half your current salary, but gives you an ownership position in the company. (This is becoming more and more common.) If you have no money in the bank and are used to spending every cent of your salary, you might not be able to take it, even though it may ultimately make you a millionaire. That would be too bad. So keep saving!

Your
Personal
Life

Tactics 45–50:

45. Marriage: Collaborate for mutual benefit
46. Advantages of being pregnant at work
47. Exercise and Jacuzzi talk: Inspire yourself to think
48. The arts: Encourage yourself to wonder
49. Friends: The world is your neighborhood
50. Lifestyle in a residential resort community

This brief chapter is offered simply to provide insight into areas in your own life that you can use to support your jumps. By giving yourself time to play and explore new interests outside of work, you'll be happier and more creative on the job.

Marriage: Collaborate for Mutual Benefit

I have the greatest husband in the world. He's mine and there's only one of him so I can't help you there. However, there are ways in which you can foster your marriage, which in turn will foster your ability to jump. For instance, my husband and I had some clear understanding from the start about how we wanted to live. We have identical backgrounds in many respects: We both studied music, we both performed in Europe, we both got MBAs (we met at Columbia), we both went to work for Citibank. We knew from the start that my corporate career was more important to me than his corporate career was to him. I like corporate work, but my husband's creativity extends through music and his own financial consulting business. When I got relocation offers, he built his portable consulting business. When I had the inflexible schedule, he got the flexible schedule. To sum it up, his career fuels my career and vice versa.

Although this worked for us, other arrangements may work better for you and your partner. The important thing is to have ongoing discussions about how your roles are changing. Come to agreements on your roles and change them whenever you need to.

Advantages of Being Pregnant at Work

Deciding when to have a child is extremely personal and complicated. Consequently, I'm going to speak about the advantages of pregnancy when you are in a stable job situation, i.e., you are not trying to leave a company or work for a new company.

Pregnancy can provide advantages to both you and your employer:

1. Most non-pregnant workers have a longer horizon to complete the job. When you're pregnant, you have to do it smarter and quicker. Take no prisoners and full throttle ahead!

2. Most non-pregnant workers do not have extended periods of wild dreams and unusually creative thoughts. If you are pregnant, you may have this opportunity. Some of your most inspired thoughts would not occur otherwise.

3. Most organizations lapse into extreme dependence on their non-pregnant leaders. When you're pregnant, your subordinates know they are going to be responsible for running the show temporarily—just the challenge they needed!

And that leads into the next stage . . . when you come back from your maternity leave, both you and your subordinates have been trained to move on to more challenging positions.

Exercise and Jacuzzi Talk: Inspire Yourself to Think

Exercise can be a coach for the mind. Running, skiing, and snowboarding are sports that work for me and I usually follow them up with a dip in the Jacuzzi. I find that exercise gives me the time to build confidence in my ideas. As I strain against the physical exercise, no one is there to disagree with my thoughts. I can go on and on agreeing with myself, visualizing the most fantastic scenario. It's not only fun to think this way, but it seems to inspire more positive thoughts and actions. It's also fun to brainstorm while exercising with other people.

The Arts: Encourage Yourself to Wonder

If you haven't learned a musical instrument or fooled around with watercolors, it's never too late to start. Like exercise, music has an expansive effect on my mind. Either while playing or listening to music, I develop a type of concentration that is useful for thinking about anything. The different melodies and musical textures help the imagination and invite new thoughts. The work it takes to learn an instrument builds confidence and concentration skills.

Friends: The World Is Your Neighborhood

I've moved so much that it takes me a year to consider subscribing to the local newspaper. Between working and being a mom, wife, daughter, and sister, sometimes my friends do not get enough of my time. Because it's always unclear how long I'll be in a particular community, I've invested less time in local friendships than many other people. If you're in a similar situation, and many jumpers are, you would probably agree that we're missing something pretty big here.

I do, however, try to keep up my national friendships through e-mail, faxing, conferences, and phone calls. Using e-mail has been great. I have running dialogues with some friends this way. Social events at conferences are another way to keep in touch with long-distance friends. I also enjoy having fun with new friends—sailing, swimming, exercising, picnicking, and partying. You can meet people who do the things you do by joining clubs.

Lifestyle in a Residential Resort Community

In a past corporate relocation, my family discovered Lake Barrington Shores, a condominium development with many recreational amenities including a lake, a marina, a golf course, swimming pools, a wildlife preserve, and a recreation center. There are about 1,300 condos in this community.

We've found that planned communities offer many advantages besides the amenities. They are a great way to meet people in your own neighborhood. In this day and age when people have less time and move more often, the clubs and gathering places offered by planned communities are a great way to become infused in a community fast. Gated communities also offer added security protection. This is nice for many reasons, including not being afraid to let your kids go outside to play and ride bikes. I also think these types of communities are good real estate investments (see Chapter Ten).

Summary

Yes, jumping can include lots of relocations and yes, they can be fun. Like anything else, your personal life gets better the more you practice changing it. Jumping can be a catalyst for improving major aspects of your life.

Part Three

People
Jumping
to the Top

12

Interviews with Executives

Professional occupations:

This book would not be complete without highlighting the careers of some individuals who are jumping to the top. Job-jumping techniques are universal for many fields and disciplines; just check out the types of careers displayed in this chapter. Each individual interviewed in this chapter has enhanced her or his career and financial future by changing jobs. You may be surprised to see how varied their success stories are—proof that many different paths lead to the top! Read on to see if the lessons they learned apply to you.

ADVERTISING

■ George F. Fencl, Jr.
Executive Vice President
Major Advertising Agency

Education

Harvard University, Dean's List, Harvard College Honorary Scholarship (four years), double major BA in East Asian Studies and Music, with honors, 1984. New York University, courses in Corporate Finance, Mergers and Acquisitions, Money Market Trading, Accounting. University of California, Berkeley, 75 percent completion toward Graduate Certificate in Marketing.

Personal

Fluent in French; some conversational Japanese and Chinese. Extensive travel in Europe (including Eastern Europe and former Soviet Union) and Middle East. Member: University Club of New York City, Harvard Club of New York City. Ray Hickok and Adams House Arms Awards for leadership, dedication, and excellence. Solo performances for music and theater; producer of various plays; awards for visual art and design. Hobbies include hang-gliding, windsurfing, weightlifting, squash, skiing.

Fencl: My undergraduate experience was perfect training for this job jumping concept. When I was a freshman at Harvard, we were advised in the first semester that 85 percent of the people who have a major in a particular area end up in a field that's unrelated to their major. They encouraged us to explore different aspects of humanity. I knew a lot about music. That freed up time for me to study something I didn't know anything about, which was Chinese culture and Chinese civilization, Chinese sociology, etc.

Hartman: Can you tell us about your first job?

Fencl: I started out at Citibank in the branches and stayed in the branches for almost three years. I spent seven months in the first branch where I started as a trainee. My training program consisted of: here's a counter where you stand, that's the door where the customers come in . . . ready . . . go! That was my training.

Then I took the job beyond just standing and answering questions. I used to find it very frustrating when the customers wrote a check for a large amount. Because the tellers could not approve it, they would come to us for approval and we couldn't find a signature card. We had no way to identify the customer. They didn't bring an ID. This happened all the time. Part of it was that our signature card files were in disarray. This became my first project: to reorganize the signature card files. This is in some ways very administrative, but it really impacted our business on a day-to-day basis.

We had 50,000 customers, so I divided up the alphabet A to Z and said this person takes letter A and this person takes letter B and everyone in the branch had an assignment to go through their letter and clean up these signature files. All of us in the branch did that over a period of time. That's the kind of thing that I did to say, "I'm not just here to stand here and answer questions, let me be active in the branch itself." Shortly after, I started applying for other positions in the bank.

My next assignment was as a management assistant in another branch. I worked through sales management and eventually became the branch manager. It was a really good experience. It exposed me to the customer and the real line operation, not the back office operation. This became my foundation for understanding consumer banking.

Hartman: Then you met the future president of Citibank's California bank. Can you tell us about that meeting?

Fencl: Both of those positions were in New York. I had met the president when I started out, maybe the second week of work. He worked at the regional processing center two or three blocks down the street. Our branch was the one where the executives would do their transactions. He noticed my Harvard ring and told me to get some experience and call him in two or three years to go out to California. He was at that very moment leaving Citibank in Queens to go to California. So I did that. About two years later, I called him up and said here's what I'm doing now. I'd like to take you up on your suggestion. This changed my job from line to staff. For the first time I really learned how an organization at the top level works.

It was an absolutely dynamite assignment. It took years out of my life. Everything was new! Even to accomplish an average level of responsibility, I had to put in an inordinate amount of hours. I had to learn how to use a PC. Most of my PC skills, which are still stronger than average today, came from that experience.

Hartman: What were some of the key projects you did that helped you to broaden your career?

Fencl: I learned the most from my responsibilities with the Executive Priority Committee meetings. I needed to coordinate, set the agenda, and report on these meetings. All the top people of the bank participated—the director of operations, the director of branch banking, the director of credit, the director of marketing, the director of treasury, the chief financial officer, etc. We had a limited budget to make systems development projects happen and the group was meant to focus the organization on which projects we would develop. It was an important function at the bank because we were building the systems from scratch.

Then I became a marketing product manager and reported to the director of marketing. I worked on database projects and also created some key projects. We were paying a vendor $50,000 to $100,000 for reports about our competitors' products. Unfortunately, all the products looked identical and the details, which were important for someone when deciding where they wanted to bank, were never part of the information that we got. So I decided to become a mystery shopper of sorts and actually go out to competitors' branches and pretend that I was a customer.

One thing that happened was a shock to me. I have a lot of respect for the California folks as marketers, but they had no clue that Bank of America was coming out with this major new push. They were announcing Saturday hours and three years' free checking and the marketing department had no idea. I established my reputation in the marketing department by saying this is a real thing. I spent my Saturdays figuring it out and found that Bank of America had opened over 100,000 checking accounts. Soon after I was promoted to marketing information manager of Citibank's National Marketing Division in Chicago.

Hartman: What was your primary motivation for this career move?

Fencl: Broader scope and higher dollars. National Marketing impacted the entire country's marketing programs instead of just

California's. I said it then and I say it now, the accumulation of talented people in Citibank's National Marketing was really quite invigorating. They had the skill, they had the motivation—all of the things that many companies don't have, they had them all.

Hartman: Why did you end up leaving this great group?

Fencl: It was a new division, and after I got there I saw the management change. I suspected Citibank was going to reorganize again. I liked the environment and yet I saw it was going to just disintegrate. At the same time I was being recruited by AIG. I left for AIG. Someone at AIG who had been an employee at Citibank and had many contacts at Citibank called up his contacts and said, "Do you know who would fit this general description?" My name was one of the top ones. So when I was in New York, I blocked out a couple of hours, interviewed, and was hired. Again, broader scope and higher dollars, but also I could see the reorganization within Citibank coming.

The focus of the AIG position was on international programs, developing programs that could be applied in any country, anywhere in the world. My responsibilities were not just in one country. National Marketing at Citibank was focused only in the United States.

Hartman: Were these marketing programs or different types of programs?

Fencl: Marketing-related and database-marketing-related specifically. The group was called American International Marketing Systems. We developed database marketing programs working with a business unit somewhere in the world, generally the United States, Europe, or Asia, and then transferred the success to other AIG businesses around the world.

After seven months, AIG closed that division and asked me to join an internal consulting group. I worked on all types of assignments, not just marketing—organizational issues, operations issues, efficiency systems. I spent two and a half years doing that. I enjoyed it but I wanted to get back to marketing. I viewed that as my main career and the company was not really increasing my skills in marketing.

Hartman: Then you were recruited by an executive recruiter?

Fencl: Yes. I joined a major advertising agency in July of 1993. I had built skills in marketing programs, communications development, and operations, but lacked sales skills. I started in sales because I viewed sales as a critical component to any company and it's an area where I did not have much experience. I started in sales but it turned out to be consulting again, which actually has been good. Perhaps my skills are more in that direction anyway.

Hartman: What types of industries do you work with?

Fencl: I'm working mostly with telecommunications or high tech and financial services. I've worked on the marketing programs for several Fortune 500 companies in these industries—on advertising, communication strategies, and channel of distribution questions.

Hartman: Do you have any advice regarding changing jobs?

Fencl: A few things come to mind. If you start out thinking it's going be a short-term assignment, you may find out that's not the case. Be prepared to live with your decision for awhile. Another piece of advice is, frankly, leave before your department gets demolished. Also develop marketable skills. Talk to people and look at the skills you are developing. Pick markets where the trend is on an upward curve and don't get so narrowly focused that you only have those skills. Keep your skills broad enough but highly marketable.

Wrapping It Up

George Fencl proves that one's career is not a spectator sport. Early on, Mr. Fencl successfully tackled hard and visible projects which others dared not touch—the signature card project, the mystery shopping project. This brought him recognition from senior management and helped him move up within the same firm. Then he gained early and continuous exposure to a broad range of senior management by assisting the head of the organization. He spent several years maximizing his scope and financial opportunities within the same company until he foresaw a massive reorganization. He propelled his career forward by jumping to an external opportunity. He went on to expand his experience beyond local and national projects to those which were international in scope. He also broadened his marketing skills to include consulting. Then that company reorganized and again an external offer provided a better opportunity. Here he acquired sales skills and experience in two additional industries. This executive is bound for glory and there is nothing that will stop him!

CHIEF EXECUTIVE OFFICER

■ Steve Price
President and Chief Executive Officer
SuperCuts
San Francisco, CA

Education

Columbia College, New York, BA in Economics, 1959. Columbia Engineering School, New York, BS in Industrial Engineering, 1960. Harvard Business School, Soldiers Field, MA and MBA with Distinction, 1963.

Other

Board of Directors, Crescent Jewelers, Inc. Board of Directors, Regis Corporation.

Hartman: You spent twenty-two years at General Foods and worked your way up to corporate vice president. Can you tell us more about your progression and some of the key moments?

Price: Although that whole experience was with one company, it helped me build a network and relationships across the entire company's staff areas, corporate areas, and line areas. It also gave me broad assignments in new fields; I didn't just move up doing the same thing.

I started out in the Maxwell House division and gained added responsibilities with positions as assistant product manager, associate product manager, product manager, product group manager, and advertising and merchandising manager and did it in a fairly traditional way but also fairly quickly.

I remember when I was promoted to product group manager, which was a senior management job in the new company. I went to see the chairman and he congratulated me for being the youngest person ever to get to that level. I said that it was a credit to the good people who mentored me, that ever since I'd come to the company, they had been more responsible for my success than I was. Then he said to me, "You mean you never worked for an incompetent son of a bitch?" I said, "No," and he said, "That's terrible! We gotta do something about that. It's very important that you do because number one, you have to learn how to react in that situation and number two, you have to see what *not* to do in a leadership position as well as what you should do." After that I was fortunate enough to work for more than one who met that qualification! That's a true story and it's funny how that stuck with me.

General Foods had bought a subsidiary, a hamburger chain called Burger Chef. It had started in Indianapolis and was a franchise as well as a company operation. The president of the operation knew me. He wanted to bring into that business classical marketing skills and also somebody with an entrepreneurial bent. I was asked and agreed to move to Indianapolis to be the executive vice president. I had several areas that reported to me, including all the stores, which were a couple of thousand stores and franchises, marketing, and all of the line operations. I moved out to Indianapolis with my wife and two little kids and spent almost three years there turning that business around.

It really broadened my perspective. This was retailing big time and it was in trouble. I had to learn a new business quickly and I had to gain credibility with the franchisees as well as all the company people. We turned that business around by doing something totally new. We upgraded the hamburger place, and made it a partial self-service restaurant. We put salad bars, condiment bars, and hostesses into the stores. We did a segmentation study, which had never been done in the business. There was a group of adults that wanted fast food, low prices, quick convenience, and good and predictable quality and service. This same group didn't want all the kids that they found at McDonald's and were frightened by the teenagers at Burger King. We found our niche there and made it a success.

I remember telling the chairman one day that the food-away-from-home business was as different from food at home as the steel business. He would have done better to buy U.S. Steel than a food-away-from-home company. General Foods subsequently sold the business to Hardee's.

The chairman asked me to become vice president of development for General Foods. This was now my third kind of career with General Foods. I headed up a development unit that acquired companies and developed new products internationally. I travelled frequently to Japan and was General Food's chief negotiator for a joint venture with a food company in Japan. We completed the national rollout of a new candy product called Pop Rocks. It was a fad and a disaster and we had to withdraw from that business.

Then I was made president of the beverage division and we introduced Crystal Light. This new diet drink was one of the biggest successes in General Foods. It still is a huge success. Many people did not think that the product could succeed; but it had a good taste and low calories, a benefit that we knew would appeal to soda drinkers.

Hartman: How did you manage to move to so many different jobs within the company? How do you do that?

Price: You do that by networking yourself with a lot of different people in the company you're in and giving them a chance to see how you can operate outside the sphere that you're in. That's one way. Another way is you stay very broad yourself. I'm always talking to people outside the business I'm in. I'm an avid reader of every newspaper and business book I can get. For example, I went to seminars on retailing before I went out to Burger Chef. I was interested in retailing because I wanted to know what made supermarkets work.

Hartman: After the twenty-two years at General Foods, why did you leave the corporate vice president job and go to Newsweek?

Price: It came to me through a large consulting firm and two partners there who had worked with me at General Foods. They had done a study for Newsweek and felt that this business needed someone who was a marketer and a good manager, but not someone who was steeped in the publishing business. They were looking for someone from outside the publishing business who would bring new ideas, new marketing, and good management skills. I was not seeking the job but agreed to have dinner with Katherine Graham to discuss it.

Hartman: Then you became executive vice president/publisher of Newsweek, Inc. In your four-year tenure there, how did you broaden your scope?

Price: Well, a couple of major things. We realigned the whole sales organization to a marketing perspective and created different versions of the magazine. The sales organization traditionally sold pages by building strong loyalties with people personally. We set up a new process where before they went out on calls they actually got research on the company in order to understand its opportunities and needs. Then they developed ideas on how General Motors, for example, could sell more cars by advertising in *Newsweek* and why that made sense. Then they made their sales calls.

The second thing we did was to create new versions of the magazine to attract new advertisers. Ninety percent of *Newsweek*'s advertising revenues were from tobacco, alcohol, and cars and I saw big problems with all three of those categories. I felt we needed new categories in order to succeed. We developed three new products called *Newsweek on Your Health, Newsweek on Your Money,* and *Newsweek on Campus,* and created a Japanese language edition of *Newsweek.*

We went to advertisers like Proctor & Gamble and said that we'd give them free advertising pages in *Newsweek on Your Health,* which was going to all dentists, doctors, and pediatricians, and be free for people to read it in their waiting rooms, if they would advertise in *Newsweek.* We put together a package buy and were tremendously successful.

Hartman: What caused you to go to Citibank and how did you make that jump?

Price: I went to Citibank to sell *Newsweek on Your Money.* I wanted Citibank to advertise in it, and so I went to three people I knew at the bank from General Foods' days. It turned out that they were looking for a high-level marketing person to join the bank. At the same time I was beginning to become concerned about my career at Newsweek. Businesspeople cannot get involved in the editorial part of the magazine. That to me is like being asked to market a product but being told you can't do anything about its formulation and packaging. The packaging was the cover and I wasn't allowed to have any input on it. I began to get frustrated because I wanted to run all the elements of the business integrated together.

Hartman: You went to Citibank for eight years to become chief executive officer of various entities in New York, Chicago, and Hong Kong. What are some of the highlights?

Price: The most exciting part, not just at Citibank but perhaps of my whole career, was running their 250 bank branches in

New York City. It's a very profitable business and Citibank's largest marketplace in the world. But the branches were not being run in a customer-driven way and the business was stalled in its growth. When I start something new, I roll up my sleeves. When I went to Burger Chef, the first thing I did was to run a store in Indianapolis at night. I did the same thing at Citibank. For the first month I ran one branch from nine to five and 250 branches from seven to nine in the morning and from five to seven at night. I closed and opened my branch every day. The tellers at that branch are still my friends. I'm sending them Christmas cards this year. I had them to my house in Connecticut for a barbecue.

In New York we developed the principles of premiere retailing. We looked at the great global retailers, such as American Express, Land's End, and Nordstrom, and put together eleven principles of retailing. The retailers understand that their customer contact people are their most important people and are their heroes. They understand that everybody from the president on down works for the tellers and for the people who deal with customers, not the reverse. Customer satisfaction is the most important thing of all.

We translated this into action plans in the branches. We created a quantitative way to measure results, which was called *SBL*—satisfying, building, and leveraging.

Hartman: I remember that at Citibank!

Price: I'm the father of SBL. We said, "Well, what do retailers do? They satisfy, they build, and they use leverage." Those three words were new vocabulary at the bank. Satisfying is very different than service. The idea of building is very different than sales. Many at the bank felt there was something demeaning about being a salesman or saleswoman but there's nothing demeaning about being a builder. Building's good stuff. They liked that. And then as opposed to productivity, which was a code word for cutting heads, we introduced the word *leveraging*. Satisfying, building, and leveraging did much more than define results; we measured them. Every quarter we had the Night of the Stars at the Hayden Planetarium. We took all 250 managers to the Hayden Planetarium and we honored those that did the best in each SBL category. It was the most exciting part of my life. When I left it was quite an emotional thing. I really didn't want to leave, but Citibank's consumer business in Hong Kong, Korea, and Taiwan really needed some of the same things. I did that in Asia. Then I came back and ran the branches for Citibank across the United States. After that I really wanted to be CEO of an entire integrated business and it wasn't possible to do that at Citibank.

Hartman: Then you accepted a position as president and chief executive officer of Crescent Jewelers in Oakland, California.

Price: Yes. Some of my contacts in the investment banking community came to me with the Crescent opportunity. It was privately owned. I got a substantial ownership stake in it and the plan was to take it public with an initial public offering in eighteen months. Within a few months of my arrival, we learned that the credit portfolio was much worse than anyone had realized. The business was in trouble, it needed financing, and the investment bankers decided to bring it closer to another publicly owned jewelry company that they controlled in Savanna, Georgia, called Freedman's. They decided to bring the CEO out who ran Freedman's and to have me work for him. The business needed the synergies of both companies. All of a sudden, six months after leaving Citibank, I found myself working for somebody else, essentially running an entity aligned with a southern jewelry company, and saying, whoops, this wasn't what my game plan was all about.

I realized that this course of action was the best way out of the financing problem of Crescent, but I decided to leave. I'm still a director today and I still have a substantial amount of stock in the company. I left and looked for what I originally came out here for. Then I started talking with SuperCuts, which incidentally came to me again through my same contacts from General Foods.

Hartman: Are you finally getting to run an integrated business?

Price: So far! I came in about twelve months ago as president/CEO to turn the business around and to report to the board. It's been fantastic and a great success. Three months ago a company called Regis came and wanted to merge with us. Regis is a large hair salon chain located in Minneapolis. There was no way to turn it down because the deal was too good for our shareholders. We have now merged, so once again I may not be running my own company, but a subsidiary of Regis. We'll see.

Hartman: Do you have any parting advice for our readers? Something that perhaps would address their concerns in trying to change jobs?

Price: If you look at each of my moves, there was always somebody involved from my past life. My advice to everybody is to build those relationships. I've got that group of ten to fifteen people who are my close, personal friends. Build that network before you need help, especially among your peers.

Wrapping It Up

Steve Price's career provides an excellent example of how to rise within one firm and then jump to top management positions of your choice. He spent twenty-two years rising to the corporate vice president level at General Foods by advancing through a broad variety of assignments across many functions. How did he manage to do this? Mr. Price networked within the firm, broadened his vision, and moved up quickly. He tackled projects with company-wide visibility, which enabled people to see his cross-functional talents. After he became a top manager, Mr. Price consistently broadened his career vistas. He accepted top management positions in a wide variety of industries, including food manufacturing, restaurants, publishing, banking, jewelry, and beauty. Mr. Price proves that a top manager can write his own ticket.

ENTREPRENEUR

■ Edward V.
  Chairman and Chief Executive Officer
  Venture-Capital-Backed Catalog Acquisitions Firm

Education

University of Illinois, Champaign, BA in Psychology and Political Science, 1975. University of Chicago, MBA in Finance and Accounting.

Personal

Hobbies: reading, music, travel. Has served on boards of symphonies, private schools, and charitable organizations such as Habitat for Humanity.

Edward: I was just starting graduate school at the University of Chicago when I received an offer from a large, privately held distributor of industrial supplies. It was the lowest of three offers I had received. They purchase, warehouse, and distribute over 200,000 different products. Their catalog consists of equipment, supplies, and maintenance and repair items such as fasteners, tools, drill presses, and abrasives, to name a few. At that time they were around $500 million in sales; they are now roughly $1.4 billion. They had a management training program and they were willing to pay for tuition if I attended school at night. So I decided to attend night school and went to work for them. It's a bit of a revolving door there, but if you make it past the first couple of cuts you're in pretty good shape. They move you around a lot; they have an interesting boot-camp type of approach.

Hartman: How did your jobs progress over your ten-year tenure with this company?

Edward: I was a management trainee and had a new position about every year and a half. They allowed me to switch back and forth between operations and finance. I spent several years in inventory- and purchasing-related positions. Then I worked my way up through management positions into corporate finance. Then I became controller for the company. It was the first time they'd put a non-CPA in as controller. I had just gotten the MBA in Finance and Accounting at the University of Chicago and that probably helped.

A few years later, I became director of physical distribution. We were going through a major expansion of our warehouse facilities from a couple hundred thousand square feet to over twice that size. I was put in charge when my predecessor was dehired over personality conflicts and performance issues.

It was quite a change for me because I went from a cushy control-type function with seventy office people reporting to me to a blue-collar environment with 250 people reporting to me. We knocked out walls, dropped in a mezzanine, put in a few miles of conveyor, and changed the systems and processes. The objective was that you should not have any downtime during the expansion project. We didn't. In the end, we were able to ship orders within an hour and thirty minutes of when they were entered and we were happy with that result.

While I was controller, I had been invited to work on some branch expansion plans with the owner and two other people. The good news about that was the visibility and understanding you gained about the business. The bad news was PCs weren't easily obtained (circa 1983) and I was generating financial statements by hand. It added several hours a night. As a word of advice, if you can get significant exposure on a project, even though it will add a huge number of hours to your week for a period of time, it's well worth it.

They told me that I was being groomed to fill my mentor's position: vice president of finance. They hinted that I might be asked to open a new branch and stay there a few years first. I was not real comfortable with the politics of that business environment. Also, I came from downstate Illinois, the country, and was getting pretty tired of Chicago's congestion. A headhunter called me about a CFO position in a $125 million construction company up in southern Wisconsin. Southern Wisconsin's beautiful, rural, and Madison is a pretty cool place given the university, state capital, etc., so I decided to take that opportunity. It was not for more money. I went for the title of vice president of finance and administration, or CFO. That was the first time I jumped to the vice president level.

Hartman: Why did you leave after only a year and a half there?

Edward: I came to the conclusion that the construction industry wasn't what I wanted. The margins were thin and the pace was not as vibrant as distribution's. Really what I wanted was to live in the Madison area, away from Chicago. Again I listened to a headhunter and about one and a half years later accepted a position at an educational supply company. I worked for this company for eight years. Similar to my first job, this company was a cataloger and distributor of equipment, supplies, and maintenance and repair items. Unlike my first company, this one distributed these products, in addition to curriculum products, to schools nationwide. There was a 30 percent jump in pay, and I became the CFO for that educational supply company. I was their first outside hire. They had venture capital behind them and they planned to buy other small educational supply companies. Within the first month, I was put in charge of all the operations because they didn't have very good operations support. Now I was CFO and VP operations. I was recruiting people from that point on. We really needed to bring in people. I moved to Mansfield, Ohio, and then to California.

Hartman: Why did you have so many moves?

Edward: One of the firms purchased by the company was starting to fall into some trouble. It was in California. They asked me to go out and run that and so I did. We had lived in Ohio a bit less than a year and then moved to California. We didn't sell the house in Ohio because we didn't know whether we could stabilize or would have to consolidate the California operation. I wouldn't know for six months. I'd have to get out there and see. We moved and it was nice because we were living in the Malibu area.

We decided to consolidate that company after all. It was an unpleasant thing because we had to dehire ninety people. The good news is we got them all jobs before we closed the doors. Although we offered them jobs in Ohio, only a few were willing to move to Ohio. We placed everyone into jobs in California by working with the state and with outplacement firms. We were real happy about that.

As a result of being out there that year, being president of that company, getting the thing consolidated cleanly, that's what led to my promotion to chief operating officer of the overall business. A year or two later, around 1993, we made an acquisition of a larger educational supply company. Combined sales were close to $180 million. This acquisition was problematic because the negotiations began in 1992 and involved a shift in control from my boss to venture capitalists. This was an involved and distracting negotiation and we were not really on our feet again as a company until 1994. Then it was a mad rush to integrate the businesses and otherwise rationalize the merger. I was made president of the platform company in Ohio, was COO for the combined companies, and was still covering the CFO function because we hadn't been able to agree on the right candidate for that job. We were really very thin (lacked executives in operations and finance and had two relatively new hires in HR and systems) while we were building new facilities, consolidating four distribution centers, putting in new computer systems, and trying to swallow a new business. It was very tough stuff and we just didn't have the kind of people we needed to have on board. We had a lot of disagreements about the timetable and what to do. We parted at the end of 1995 and I started my own company with a longtime friend and colleague.

Hartman: What is your business now?

Edward: We're doing two things. First, to keep food on the table, we're consulting to the catalog industry. Between my partner and myself, we've got almost 40 years of catalog experience. We have both consumer and business-to-business catalog companies calling us and asking for help, especially in operations. We have experience in three very different industries. We both had industrial supply in our background. I then went into institutional (the school supply company) and he went into consumer. Between the two of us, we have three different industry segments covered.

Primarily though, we are looking for acquisitions. We now have some venture capital money behind us. We have a business plan with the charter to go out and buy small- to medium-sized industrial supply companies which are in certain niches. That's what happened in the consumer business in the 1970s and 1980s and we feel it's about to happen in the business-to-business side in the 1990s and beyond. We think there's an incredible opportunity there. The venture money we've talked to agree, so they've pledged a certain amount of money for us. Now we are trying to line up the appropriate targets.

Regarding consulting, we work cooperatively with others who are doing consulting and who have been in the industry for a long time. They may or may not jump on board the acquisitions when we get those lined up. In many ways we are all independent contractors.

Hartman: You've moved from a corporate environment to that of an entrepreneur. Are you glad you did it? Do you wish you'd done it sooner? Do you have any regrets or any further advice to people?

Edward: I tried doing it twice before. In fact, I forgot to mention this, when I came back from the California situation, I wasn't happy with the decision to reduce the merchandising staff from fifteen to two, among other things, so I quit. They asked me to stay on for a few months while we tried to work through transition issues. That's when they offered me the COO job and more money. During that time I was trying to get another business venture going. The only offer of advice I can suggest is that I don't think it's possible, at least I wasn't able, to take a serious plunge at an outside business while still being employed full-time by a corporation.

Hartman: The only way you could do it was to quit?

Edward: Yes. That's a tough move for most people. It was tough for me. Very hard. You look at it and say here's my savings, here's everything I have. How long can I work for myself before I have to go get hired?

Hartman: What helped you do it?

Edward: I don't think I was ready or would have been ready to just go do this had I not tried it on my own, part-time, a couple of times before. I also think that if you're going to partner with some venture capital and actually do a formal business plan, you really need to have at least eighteen months of savings. Another thing that helped is that I went to Stanford a couple of summers ago. It's a great program and it's a good review of things you may have studied years before.

Wrapping It Up

Many of us dream of becoming entrepreneurs, but Edward took the leap and did it. He teaches us that this career move requires preparation and practice. Edward built his skills through a ten-year ascent within his first company. Then he jumped to an external opportunity for a more marketable title and broader responsibilities, not dollars. Then he jumped externally again for a top management title and that's when the dollars also increased. After reaching that level, Edward made an attempt to go out on his own. But this is the type of leap that takes practice. He went back to work, saved enough money to make a bigger leap, and then tried again. Edward is now CEO of his own firm with venture capital backing and staff.

MARKETING

■ Loren Smith
Consultant
Former Chief Marketing Officer, U.S. Postal Service

Education
Albion College, AB.University of Michigan, MBA, 1960.

Personal
Bicycling, motorcycle riding, piloting, fly fishing, skiing; studying voice, performing as a soloist; vice chair Council for Basic Education, Washington, D.C.

Smith: The first job I had was with Colgate Palmolive Company, New York City. I was about the third MBA they ever hired and they were in a turnaround situation. I had offers from Proctor & Gamble, General Mills, Firestone, Colgate Palmolive, and a couple of local companies in Michigan. What I concluded was that, coming out of a graduate program, you ought to go to a place that had a lot of resources, had a lot of recognized problems, and did not think that they had the solutions for them.

Hartman: How long did you spend there?

Smith: I was there five years, from 1960 to 1965. During that period of time, I started off with a brief sales experience and then moved into product management. About three years into my career, I got a chance to work as executive assistant to the chairman. That's where I learned to manage from macro goals that exceeded the capacity of the existing organization.

Colgate was an interesting situation in that its domestic business was quite weak. Although sales were split evenly, ninety percent of their profits were from overseas and 10 percent were from the United States. Then the new chairman of the board went to Wall Street with his announcement to invest $22 million a year in the development of new products domestically. He also committed to grow the profits of the whole business by 10 percent a year, and the U.S. business by at least 20 percent a year. He provided ground rules. We couldn't spend the $22 million on the existing products, but the $22 million had to come from the existing products.

As a result, Colgate pioneered the use of a variety of marketing techniques. We pioneered short-length commercials and the buying of spot television, as opposed to heavy reliance on network shows. We were one of the first ones to invest heavily in women's sports because women were our customers. We sponsored the Dinah Shore Women's Golf Tournament.

One of the new categories we actually invented was the Baggies Food Wrap business. In those days people didn't believe that you could put food in plastic and have it not get tainted. We went to a company that made plastic on a roll for dry cleaners and developed Baggies. We started off with the sandwich bag and the utility bag and revolutionized the wrap business. We had a joint venture with a manufacturer because we couldn't put any capital into it and we became the marketing arm.

Along about 1965, I got some advice from a friend that I've actually used in my career ever since. He said ask yourself three questions:

1. Do you like what you're doing?
2. Are you learning anything?
3. Is it leading anywhere?

I wasn't ready to bet on a new chairman coming in to replace the one that had turned the company around and I had finally gotten to the point where I couldn't answer yes to two of those three questions. On two different occasions, Ogilvy and Mather tried to hire me; they were not one of Colgate's agencies. I turned them down and said to their vice chairman that I really thought I was still better off in a job that was disposing of decisions rather than recommending them. They said if you ever decide you're going to leave, call us and we'll introduce you to some of our clients. Well, that's exactly what I did.

They introduced me to the executive vice president (and later president) of General Foods. General Foods brought me in to set up a new products function in the coffee business. After about a year and a half, I was made the advertising manager over all the coffees. This was a reasonably influential job at that point in time because we contributed about 55 percent of General Foods' profits. I did that for three years.

Then in 1970, General Foods discovered that they had made several acquisitions, none of which had been researched very well and all of which were in trouble. They also wanted to acquire new marketing capabilities like direct marketing and direct sales. I was given a chance to go out and run a direct selling cosmetic company in California as chairman and CEO. I spent the next four years discovering that it was really more of an illegal pyramid plan and it needed to be substantially turned around. There were a variety of problems associated with that but in the end General Foods decided to divest from it.

I decided that I didn't want to run more businesses for big companies and I started my own consulting business. I did that from the back of a bus that my wife and I decided we'd live in for a year. We sold our house in Bel Aire, which was a very cushy area of Los Angeles. We got this thirty-four-foot bus, put a V.W. on the back of it, an electric typewriter inside it, and put our three kids on a home study program. We set out to experiment with me starting a consulting business and the family living in small towns near the ocean or in the mountains.

Hartman: You'd move the bus around?

Smith: We gave ourselves a year to discover where we'd like to live and see if we liked living there. We had a rather long, painful, democratic process that ended up with us circling five areas on a map of the United States that we thought were the kind of areas where we'd like to live. Then we headed to those areas. We actually lived in four of them before we made up our mind where we were going. During that process, I started consulting.

I found that companies that did not have strong marketing capabilities turned out to be the most eager clients. I ended up with hospital management firms, oil well drilling companies, a restaurant business, and Citibank.

Citibank crossed my radar screen in 1978, when John Reed was a group vice president. Four years earlier he'd set up the consumer banking business and he wanted to make the whole thing more market driven. When I was introduced to him, I asked him what that meant. He said that when he went to Philip Morris board meetings, they would discuss brand positioning, relative share of market, competitive strategy, and that sort of thing. When he went to Citibank board meetings, they would discuss excess computer capacity and credit losses. One seemed to be talking about the factory and the other always seemed to be talking about the customer.

Four of us helped John build one of his four core courses for his business managers. His concept was to train people to manage credit and risk from a bank standpoint and three other key disciplines: managing people, managing technology, and managing marketing and growth. The four of us built the marketing and growth course that was core curriculum for all the business managers. It was eventually given to about 3,000 managers who ultimately made up the senior management ranks of the consumer business at Citibank. Between 1978 and 1985, Citibank became my largest client worldwide. I assisted them in everything from their traveler's check business to companies in the Philippines, Taiwan, Europe and the Middle East, and the United States.

Then, circumstances in my life changed. I became tired of traveling and had gone through a divorce so I was freer to relocate. In 1985 I took a full-time job with Citibank in New York.

Hartman: Why did you go back to a big firm?

Smith: In the end, life is your career, not the other way around. At some point in time, you stand back and decide to put some roots down. You decide to be in a town more than four days in a row and build friends and roots in a community. It also fit with my three questions . . . I could learn a lot, have a lot of fun, and it would lead somewhere.

I went to New York to be Citibank's general manager in charge of marketing and new product development. I was there at the start-up of computer banking, called Direct Access. Then I became part of a group that was interviewing people to go out and be the next chairman of the failed savings and loan in Chicago. We were not finding the kind of entrepreneurial spirit we wanted. I was asked to go out and run it.

In 1987, I went out to Chicago to become chairman of the savings and loan, which we then proceeded to turn into the leading consumer bank in Chicago. In 1989, I was asked to set up a national marketing division that would be the primary driver of both new products and marketing for all the consumer banking business. We set that up. Then in 1991, there was new senior management at the bank and they weren't particularly interested in having a national marketing division. They asked if I'd go back to New York.

By 1993, I was back to my three questions: Did I like what I was doing? Was I learning anything? Was it leading anywhere? And it became pretty clear that it was probably time to go back to my consulting business and retire from Citibank. So

I did that. Along the way I decided to get remarried and discovered Taos, New Mexico. I had built a house in Taos. I am a big skier and like hiking, biking, and river rafting even more. So it's got me covered all year round out there. I set up shop out in Taos, kept an apartment in New York for a while, and went back into consulting. My goal was to consult about one-third of the time, work with not-for-profits about one-third of the time, and goof off one-third of the time. I could afford to do that.

I started consulting to the U.S. Postal Service in 1994, and got seduced by the business. It's a marvelous institution with gigantic challenges. I gave the postmaster general, Marvin Runyan, a handshake that I would come work with his team to see if I couldn't get them to be more market driven and customer focused. We did a lot. I did that for about as long as government bureaucracy could tolerate an entrepreneur and that brings you up to today.

Hartman: Could you provide any advice regarding negotiating compensation?

Smith: One of the observations I've made is that if you're working just to get paid, you've probably got the wrong motivation. I was driven early on by wanting to run the biggest company I could get my hands on at the earliest age. You might say I was driven by wanting power and control. I wanted to prove my ideas, rise and fall with my ideas. I didn't have any capital so I had to do it within big businesses. I discovered along the way that if you were successful, people would come by and dump wheelbarrows full of money on you. I also discovered that if you helped your company grow and the stock got better that that was a way to get rewarded.

Hartman: Do you have any other thoughts you'd like to give us? Any regrets? How did you feel about making all these job changes?

Smith: Yeah, I can think of several things. When you have multiple careers, you have to have an attitude toward continual learning. You provide value for employers by being on the leading edge of new things. Most people frankly aren't. Most people repeat today what they did yesterday and get very lazy in terms of the need to go out and learn new things. If you're constantly learning new things, you're constantly increasing your value to the people who put you to work.

That said, I think there's a real danger if you hop too much. You need to stay in places long enough to see the consequences of your decisions. You need to see your failures as well as your successes. You should live through the cycles of the business you're in and not just come in for a portion of it.

Wrapping It Up

Loren Smith proves that a capable executive can rise to the top of corporations and work independently as a consultant. After only three years on his first job out of school, he became assistant to the chairman of a major corporation. This early exposure enabled Mr. Smith to build his skills on sizable, high visibility projects. After five years with his first firm, he jumped to an external opportunity that offered broader responsibilities and perspectives. Then he jumped to start his own consulting business. His next jumps alternated between senior management positions and consulting on his own. It seems to be like this— your career is a bus. Sometimes you drive it. Sometimes you ride in it. Sometimes it's full of people and sometimes it isn't. But wherever you go on that journey, it's important that you like what you're doing, are learning lots, and know where you're going.

NON-PROFIT

■ Christine P.
Vice President
Non-Profit Educational Corporation

Education

Maryland State University, BS, 1974. Illinois State University, MA in Education, 1984.

Christine: I started with a bachelor's of science degree and on completion of that I was trained in park administration. Then I got a job as recreation supervisor. I worked there for eight years and it was a very fulfilling time. I was never doing the same thing twice; I had lots of different community recreation programs to run. I would have liked to have continued; however, it was time that I step up and go back to school. I had mastered this job. I wanted to get a master's degree and be a director. I wanted to have a more responsible position where I would understand financial management, accounting practices, and the business side of things.

I gave them eight good years; I felt really good about that. I think part of your work is to feel good. I always asked myself, "How much am I giving back to this company and to this community?" I looked around at some of my peers who were only with their park district maybe four years or less. But sticking around longer worked well for me. I could give them eight years. Not only that but all the rest of my life I've been able to go back to that foundation and ask for references. I was a person they won't forget, and that has helped me in every job I've gotten since.

Hartman: Where did you go after getting your master's degree?

Christine: I became the community education director for a small city in Minnesota, a job I held for four years. I was directly responsible for maintaining the budget. I also was responsible for maintaining school facilities during the off hours—evenings, holidays, and summers. I worked with principals, administrators, and superintendents and was involved in bigger decision making, which required some maturity. I had to have their respect and they had to have mine. I also worked on community organizations, representing our community education department. As part of the job, I spoke publicly to promote our programs, missions, and goals. This experience helped build my confidence in my stand-up presentation skills and my leadership role.

Hartman: You became a leader in this community; it was much more of a public role than your past job.

Christine: Yes, and I learned a lot. I made mistakes. I just looked at the mistakes as a learning opportunity and didn't let too much get me down. I really liked the leadership role and really liked standing up in front of people and rallying them to the group's cause. I also took courses that would help me on the job; one was public relations and another was public speaking.

Then one day a company that specializes in training saw me speak at a meeting. They asked if I would like to be a trainer for them. So a company came to me while I was doing what I liked to do. But it was out of my field. It was not community education, nor park and recreation—no community projects and kids. I was going to be a professional person doing professional training. I gave that some serious thought. It was a nice promotion, a challenge, and I decided to take it. They trained me, sending me around to different states to observe their training. Then I did training for them for about a year.

Then I used my passion for customer service and took on contracts for a few years. I trained the employees of a regional group of Holiday Inns in their First Concern program: "customer service is our first concern." In that opportunity I was able to create incentive programs for all the employees so that they felt the importance of treating their customers well. I also had a contract with a local training firm. Contract-type jobs worked well for me. I preferred to lead myself and determine the job. I liked to figure out how much time it would take to do the job and then figure out what they would pay me for it.

Next I decided to take all the skills I had learned about customer service and design my own business, Profiles. I took everything I knew about customer service and I designed a questionnaire. I did private service surveys for hotel companies like Hyatt, Hilton, and Holiday Inn. Just like a mystery shopper, I would come in and stay at the hotel. Then I'd create a profile for the manager and rate their customer service. I had a scale with a 5-point rating, a 4-point rating, and so on. I would also let them know how they compared to their competition.

This business gave me a lot of freedom to go out and travel, which is what I wanted to do. I wanted to see the world and stay in different places. I was single. I created jobs that enabled me to travel, eat fancy food, play golf, go swimming, and basically do all the things that I like to do! It was great. I would have continued at that; the business was taking off.

At that point, I met my husband and we got married. He didn't like the idea of me traveling and going to all these great places without him. I can understand that. And then I became pregnant and my career, at that point, ended. I sold the business and I became a mom.

In the first year with my son, I wanted to have a little part-time job out of the home. I joined World Book Encyclopedia. I saw an ad in the paper and thought, "I can do that, I can sell World Book." I ended up staying with that for about six years. I sold World Books to other moms in the neighborhood. The reason I wanted to sell encyclopedias was because (1) I wanted to meet other moms with young children; (2) I wanted to get back in the educational field; (3) I wanted to regulate my own time so that I could be at home or bring my children with me; and (4) I wanted to make a little money so that I could contribute financially to the household.

I made quite a bit of money and moved up the ladder to the position of district manager, which involved hiring, training, supervising, and coming up with incentives. So I was applying my skills and putting it all into action for World Book. Then World Book started changing in their strategy and began selling computer software. I'm not a strong salesperson when it comes to computers. It's just not me, so I ended my position with World Book.

I sat down at the drawing table and decided to put all my skills down on paper, all the things I liked to do that I can do well and that I could offer to a company. Again I decided to start my own company. That's how I came up with this educational company that I've been running for three years.

Hartman: How would you describe this company?

Christine: The primary mission is to help poor people around the world by marketing their handicrafts. The second mission is to educate our young kids on the cultures of the world and the people who make up these cultures. This company develops, markets, and teaches social studies curriculums. The curriculums are in the form of "teaching baskets." Each basket is from one country and contains gifts of twenty-five to thirty crafts, instruments, and artifacts made in that country. We develop stories, music, and art activities related to each gift that help children learn about the people in that culture. We have three major teaching baskets: the African, the Latin American, and the Asian. We're also developing a smaller series called the village craft series.

This company has taken off. After only two years, a Fortune 500 company wanted to buy the teaching-basket concept from us. We decided not to sell it to them. Instead, we made them an exclusive line to resell. We held back to keep our company non-profit. We now have five full-time employees, a warehouse, and many schools as our clients. We also go out to the schools and teach children about other cultures. I also do programs for teachers.

This company has been a good lifestyle choice for me too. I wanted to do something that was educationally meaningful to children and I had a passion and a concern for people in developing countries who were hungry and poor and struggling. I also wanted to do something that my kids could participate in. My children travel with me to the foreign countries and have provided ideas for the teaching baskets. They also enjoy providing ideas for the curriculum activities.

Hartman: Would you like to give us an idea of how this company contributes to your household income?

Christine: Our household is supported by two incomes. My income has grown steadily and in the future will surpass my husband's in earnings. In the future we look to my career for the bigger income. But I wouldn't do that until my kids are older and they don't need me at home. As a parent, I want my kids to realize that they can always come to me, that I'll always be there for them. I'll always be their advocate, no matter what.

Hartman: Do you have any advice to give regarding changing jobs?

Christine: Don't be afraid of going out there and selling your gifts and your qualities. Be really enthusiastic and confident. When people are hiring, that's what they're looking for. They want someone really confident, solid, and who has an ability to communicate. Believe it or not, you're probably more talented than you give yourself credit for.

Of all the things I've done, probably in my heart I didn't think I was really qualified—but I wasn't going to let them know that. I was going to go in and know I could do the job. Even if I wasn't able to do it right now, I could do it if they would just give me the chance and the training. I was a willing learner. I did what it takes to get it done. I've never been a person that is nine to five. Never. I work at what the job needs to get done. I take it home with me, I work weekends, I just work to accomplish the job.

Wrapping It Up

If you are a hard-driving business type, you need to shift perspectives in order to learn from Christine's career. Recognize that this woman's career perfectly matches her current priorities in life—lots of time with family first, business second. Christine is in the non-profit industry and is motivated more by caring for people than by her own personal career or money. Christine enjoyed her first jobs because they enabled her to contribute to her community. Then she created a highly successful non-profit business, which she does as a part-time job. She involves her children in the business and is careful not to let the business grow past the time she has for it. This person is happy because she has satisfied her career priorities.

ORGANIZATIONAL DEVELOPMENT

■ Barbara Wiley
  Manager, Organizational Development
  Major Food Products Company

Education

University of Kansas, BA in Human Resources, 1976. University of Kansas, MA in Public Administration, 1986.

Personal

Member, Association for Quality and Participation, American Society for Training and Development. Hobbies: travel, gourmet cooking, herb gardening, reading.

Wiley: When I think about taking a new job I ask myself three questions and need to be able to give myself these answers:

1. Have I ever done it? *No.*
2. Will it kill me? *No.*
3. Does it look interesting? *Yes.*

I started out putting myself through undergraduate school working at a clerical job for the state of Kansas. After I got my degree I continued working for the state as an employment manager of a university medical center. My interview presented a challenge. I was speaking with this group of people who ended up being my peers and I remember saying, "Wait a minute, you're asking me to take on this job and you want me to have the responsibility for this group of people but I won't actually supervise them? So, I'll have all the responsibility but I won't have the authority?"

Hartman: What did they say?

Wiley: They said that's the way it is. Well, very interestingly one of them called me at home that night, kind of embarrassed, and said, "We talked to the director and actually those people will report directly to you."

In any job I believe we all want responsibility, accountability, and authority. I gained the responsibility for the recruitment and orientation of 5,000 professionals and the authority to supervise employment interviewers and the clerical staff.

Although I worked for the state, I wanted more responsibility as quickly as possible. I stayed for two years at that job and then was the personnel director at a state youth center for two years. Then I became a personnel manager in the state department of administration and worked there for four years. I wrote personnel regulations for all state employees. I also had responsibility for putting on a conference for all the personnel officers in the state. It was for about 100 people and I had no budget. I figured out how to do it anyway. I talked to people and asked, "Would you be willing to come talk? I can't give you any money, but it might be an opportunity." If they were a consultant, I'd say, "You might end up with some consulting business."

I asked a man to speak at the conference who had also spoken to my graduate school class. As we were leaving, I told him how impressed I was with his organization and said that it would be a wonderful place to work. "If you ever have an opening give me a call." Then he said, "That's really interesting because we do have an opening." This job was a significant shift in my career. I went from wearing nice dress-up girl clothes from eight to five in an office, Monday through Friday, to being a frontline supervisor, a team leader, working second shift in a dog food factory.

Hartman: In a dog food factory?

Wiley: Making dog food. Wearing jeans, steel-toed shoes. Suddenly the people I worked with didn't wear hose and ties and many of them had tattoos.

Hartman: Did this job have something to do with human resources?

Wiley: This is the Gaines Pet Food Plant in Topeka, Kansas. Twenty-five years ago they started self-directed work teams; it's the grandfather of all self-directed work teams. This is an organization that is doing neat stuff. There are many people that think "How on earth did you go from state government to manufacturing?" Again, I thought, "Have I ever done it? *No;* Will it kill me? *No;* Does it look interesting? *Yes.*"

Hartman: So how long did you stay there?

Wiley: After two years the company was purchased by Quaker Oats. They were looking for someone who had training experience and frontline supervision in manufacturing. I held my hand up. They asked me to come to their headquarters, which happened to be in Chicago. So, here I am, Dorothy in Kansas, and she's asked to go to the big city. I will never forget walking down the main drag, Michigan Avenue, my first day on the job. Nothing in my life is the same. Everything has changed. Every single thing I am doing today is different—the clothing I'm wearing, where I'm living, everything. It was just amazing.

Hartman: I've also experienced that sensation when life changes so quickly. I had the sensation of watching myself in a movie; it was happening so fast I wasn't entirely feeling it.

You spent nine years at Quaker Oats starting as a management trainer and ending as a manager of team development. What were the highlights?

Wiley: I was doing manager training out of their corporate headquarters for their manufacturing plants. I was doing projects such as train the trainer, cost reduction, creating performance standards. Then I had the opportunity to develop a teamwork system for a brand new manufacturing plant that the company was building in Kentucky. It was supposed to be an eighteen-month lateral assignment and then who knew what was going to happen after that.

I might add, my husband had been moving around with me on all these jobs and having to find new jobs himself. When we went to Chicago, he found a job about 200 miles away, so we lived in two cities for about three and a half years and saw each other only on the weekends. I'm not recommending that. We're together eighteen years as of yesterday. The reason I bring it up is that I wasn't willing to go to Kentucky without him. We decided to give up his income, which was 60 percent of our income at the time.

Hartman: Was the opportunity so great that it was worth it?

Wiley: Yes. I had an opportunity to help build something from scratch and do it right. I had become very interested in high-performance organizations and self-directed work teams. I had done lots of reading and work on that. My master's thesis had been on an innovative volunteer organization that I was involved with. I had become very interested in trying to design organizations to be not only more productive, but a better place for people to be. It was the right thing to do so, hey, don't ask me twice.

Hartman: What did you do after that?

Wiley: That stretched out into about three and a half years. Frankly, I saw some handwriting on the wall that there was going to be some downsizing in the company and at the same time I got an interesting call from a recruiter. Later someone told me, boy you really read the tea leaves well, because many of the people I worked with ended up being laid off.

I went to Orlando, Florida, and became the director of organizational development for Red Lobster. They were owned by General Mills at the time. The company wanted to deploy self-directed work teams in 600 restaurants around the country. This was a huge challenge and my first one that was national in scope. At first when the recruiter called, I said, "Florida's hot, I have no intention of going to Florida, good-bye." They called back and said, "Wait, wait, wait." I went there because the job interested me, but for the two and a half years I was there, I hated Florida. After a couple of years the company went through some major changes and I began to think about a new assignment. I thought, if I'm going to put a lot of energy into doing something new, I'd rather do it in a climate and environment that I really like. So my husband and I started looking at the Midwest and West. I really think my heart is more in manufacturing and I like food manufacturing. This new job as manager of organizational development broadens my responsibilities to work in a unionized manufacturing environment.

Hartman: Is there anything, advice or regrets, you'd like to provide about changing jobs?

Wiley: One regret is that I should always have trusted my instincts. There are a couple of times when I knew in the first six months that it was not a good move for me and I should have left. I should have cut my losses and left then. When that happened I ended up making lemonade out of lemons. But it was at great personal cost and a lot of stress. It didn't need to be that way.

Just the other day, a friend called and had been at a new company for three months. She said, "You know it's just not working but I really ought to give it. . . ." I said, "No, you have worked a variety of places, you are good, you know it's not working, and it's not going to suddenly get better. If this is not the job they hired you for, then leave." She interviewed and she has gotten in on the ground floor of something that sounds like it is going to be wonderful.

Wrapping It Up

Smart and bold! If it won't kill her, and she's never done it, and it looks interesting, Barbara Wiley will go for it. Here is a woman who started out as a secretary to pay for college and has reached the level of middle manager in a major corporation. How did she do it? Ms. Wiley built her skills but also seized the moments to change jobs. When she sensed her opportunity to become a manager, she spoke up and grabbed it. When an excellent external offer appeared, she jumped! So what if it's work in a dog food factory? It gave her line experience in the field of organizational development. Then zap, back into the suit, for another external offer doing management training in manufacturing plants nationwide. Layoffs didn't bother Ms. Wiley. Each time she jumped before they happened to other external offers in middle management. Ms. Wiley is an executive who soars.

SALES

■ John B.
Director, New Product Development
National Market Research Firm

Education

Indiana University College of Arts and Sciences, BA in Economics with a minor in Marketing, 1983.

John: I worked all throughout high school. I started out as a stock boy for a retail chain of department stores. At sixteen, I went on the floor in sales. I took college prep courses, left high school at one o'clock, and spent the afternoon working. I graduated mid-term and took twelve hours of college before I had technically graduated from high school.

Hartman: Where did you work your first job out of college?

John: A small regional agency, with $50 million in billing, outside of Minneapolis. I was a field account executive. I started in client service. The original Pizza Hut account.

Hartman: How long did you work for them?

John: Eleven to twelve months. Then I went to a regional market research company on the client services side as a project director. I wanted exposure to larger, blue-chip companies. I wanted to be in an environment that was objective; it's either right or it's wrong. Market research is a little more objective than advertising, which is very subjective. This wasn't sales yet, but as project director you're doing everything but cutting the deals.

Hartman: Why did you leave?

John: After three years I was looking for better analytical consulting and methods for qualitative and quantitative market research. I also felt that I could earn more elsewhere. I went to a smaller market research and consulting firm.

Hartman: Why did you leave after staying there two years?

John: I decided to get into real estate sales. I got my real estate license, moved back to Indiana from Chicago, and tried that for about fifteen months. I was a real estate broker selling commercial real estate. As a commercial real estate firm, we had a service that provided market analyses for potential sites. This interested me more than real estate sales and it related to my background. I decided to pursue the suppliers to this market research, and get into the secondary side of data and research. I'd previously been on the primary side.

Then I became an account executive with a national research supplier of secondary data—the same supplier that had provided the site location research. I was there three years and in my third year made 250 percent of my quota. Although I had done unusually well, I ran into a political roadblock and was fired. I also went through a divorce.

I took a forty-five-day interim assignment working for a small market research consulting firm while I looked for another job. Within two months of the firing, I landed an account executive job for a competitor to the national research supplier.

Hartman: You did well, you were not rewarded for it, and you went directly to a competitor. You worked three years for the competitor. Could you help us understand what advantages you brought to the competitor and also how that benefited you personally?

John: I had a much better understanding of the industry than my counterparts at the competing firm. I had just come from the competitive side. I had a huge advantage because I understood the competitive advantages of each firm and their products. When you come from a competitor, you're worth ten times whatever they pay you. They also used my input in marketing strategy and strategy development. They got perks beyond what they paid for.

Hartman: You worked for three years and then went to another major competitor in the same industry.

John: I had six years experience in the industry with some of the top competitors. I found this made me more valuable to the other competitors. I went to another major competitor for much higher pay and broader responsibilities. I started out in sales again but after six months they promoted me to director of new product development. Most positions are defined in a very constrained way. This position has the best of both worlds. It's new product development but with both marketing and sales components to it. I'm commissioned on the entire division's sales for the new products I develop. It's very exciting!

Hartman: How did you negotiate this promotion after only six months with this company?

John: I started in sales with a group that was growing and really just sold my boss on the position that I have now. It was designed from the ground up by me. Both in terms of what the expectations are and the compensation, it's quite a custom job. I also think the flat organization helped. There's not a lot of bureaucracy—my boss is the president of the division and she can do what she wants. I had done a superb job for the first six months and I saw a market need so I brought this job idea to my boss. Although I don't regard negotiations as a large strength of mine, I renegotiated after six months because they needed new products to satisfy the market demand. I was the best person here for new product development because of my knowledge of the industry. I had already proven myself, thought they'd go for it, and they did.

Hartman: Is there any advice on changing jobs that you would like to provide?

John: My last two job changes have been kind of forced decisions. They weren't really my choice. It comes a point where you either run into a wall or you run into some personality that is constrictive—a different management style or whatever. That's particularly true in sales management. Sales is often just run by the numbers, not for how much somebody knows or can contribute. However, especially in sales of research and secondary data, this management style doesn't make sense. We're not selling widgets out there. There's so much more that you do beyond just the numbers. Most organizations fail in that they treat and think of salespeople as number crunching, number pushing, widget salespeople and that's really stupid.

Hartman: What should they be doing?

John: Companies should value a salesperson in a number of ways. Look at his repeat business and percentage of growth within the account base and measure the satisfaction of his clients. The salespeople's ideas should be channeled into marketing strategy and new product development—they are on the front line and understand customer needs.

Hartman: Do you have any advice for people contemplating a job change?

John: When you're on the verge of changing jobs, you have more power than you realize, especially because you are new to the company. Most company organizations are dysfunctional. You don't see that on the outside when you're interviewing. It's like buying a car. You don't see all the negatives of the car until you've had it for six months. Well a car is very similar to a corporation. They all have their dark little secrets, generally in personalities and management of the organization, which you don't see unless you work there.

When you come from the outside, particularly from a competitor, you add a lot to the organization. They need the new blood. You can add so much to that environment. New blood managed correctly and channeled efficiently makes a lot of changes to the old organization. That's exactly what they need.

Wrapping It Up

John's career is a good example of a jumper who transforms the future. He unabashedly jumped through jobs with three competitors in the same industry and then became director of new product development. Of course! Who else would better know what products that industry needed? Because he jumped at a fast rate to external offers every one to three years, he was used to being the new guy and felt that it was an advantage. He saw that companies need to change to benefit by market conditions and claimed that as part of his job. The more the company wanted to change, the more they liked John. His latest jump up is as a change agent for his company and industry.

TECHNOLOGY

■ Sally L.
Consultant
Big Six Management Consulting Firm

Education

University of California, BA in Political Science (minor in Computer Science), 1983.

Sally: The first job I had was as a programmer for a company that did time-sharing. This was in the days when computing equipment was not accessible to most companies. It wasn't easy for companies to buy computers, so they had this service known as time-sharing. The time-sharing company would have salespeople who would go out and sell contract programming services to customers such as AT&T. I worked for a company that had a mainframe and programmers all over the country. The programmers dialed up to the computer via modem and did programming in FORTRAN.

I was there for less than a year. I felt that I was doing better work than people who were more senior and getting paid more than me. I asked them for a raise after six months and they wouldn't give me one. Consequently, I left to go to a company that did very similar work for 50 percent more money.

Hartman: Did you jump purely for money or was there any other reason?

Sally: It was money.

Hartman: How long did you stay at the next company?

Sally: For less than a year. They disappointed me in a couple of ways. They weren't coming through with the right training. There were opportunities to learn C and UNIX and they were giving this training to other people who had been there longer. By this time I had learned much more about this profession. I had learned how to program. I had learned about systems analysis and project level skills. Rather than just working on an individual program, I was working on whole systems.

Then I went to work for a small entrepreneurial start-up company and was there for seven years, a long time. I started with a 35 percent raise.

Hartman: So money was part of this jump as well?

Sally: Yeah, but also a chance to have a little more freedom. Traveling was interesting to me then. I wouldn't take a job for the same reason now.

I ended up learning a lot about marketing and customer service in this job. I was constantly dealing with customers. I was doing a lot of trade shows. Between the customer support and public speaking, I developed an iron constitution. I was growing the company and supporting myself. I was the fifth employee and we grew to over thirty people. This built my confidence.

But I knew that my growth was limited there. I had to figure out a way to get a job at equal or better pay. My most transferable skill was my knowledge of configuring networks of UNIX systems. It was more of a career switch than a career advancement at that point. I went more into support than developing software. It was a defensive play at that point.

Hartman: What do you mean by that?

Sally: At this point I had bought a house in the New York metropolitan area and there wasn't a lot of opportunity for a manager of CAD CAM programmers.

Hartman: Did you have very rare skills?

Sally: Right.

Hartman: Okay, so you wanted to take a job where you would learn more marketable skills?

Sally: Right. I went to a Wall Street firm and managed their help desk.

Hartman: How long did you stay there?

Sally: Less than a year. I jumped to another Wall Street financial firm in a similar job but at a more technical spot. I also found that the managerial part of the support job was stressful. I wanted something that was more technical, more marketable, and less involved in management. So that's what I did at the new Wall Street firm, UNIX systems administration—engineering work. I felt that that would help me in the long run.

Hartman: You were there for two years. Were these marketable skills?

Sally: They were very marketable. It was getting to the point where they weren't really doing very interesting types of things at this company. They were very conservative in terms of what they implemented. I felt that my talents were being wasted.

Hartman: You left to find intellectual challenge. Was there any other reason?

Sally: I also decided that I didn't really like permanent employment. I went into consulting for a big six management consulting firm. I've been here for about a year. I find the idea that not being expected to remain in one place for a long time takes a lot of pressure off of me.

Hartman: Why is that? Could you describe what you mean by the pressure?

Sally: Well, there's an assumption that when you're employed full-time, you are going to be there forever and that leaving is some type of sin. There's the whole loyalty factor that is very, I don't know if dishonest is the right word, perhaps unrealistic.

Hartman: Now that you are a consultant, how is it different?

Sally: It is understood that you are there to do a project. Your assignment is limited; although a lot of places will keep renewing you year after year. But if you decide you've had enough and you want to move on, you just do it.

Hartman: Is it a freer feeling?

Sally: Yes. It's really a matter of personality. Some people like to get in an organization and get to know everyone and move their way on up and stay in the same place for a long time. Some people, like me, just like to be able to know that if things don't work out, you can move on. If I find that I'm not growing intellectually and financially, I'd rather find another project that's more suitable. Sometimes you need to change companies to do that.

Although I work for only one consulting firm, I can work on a series of projects for different companies. I'm not an independent consultant, although that is the next step. If I make the right contacts or get a good customer or team up with other consultants, I'll go independent.

Hartman: Do you have any advice or regrets regarding changing jobs?

Sally: Don't try this at home! Seriously, speaking about work, the grass is always greener on the other side. I made a lot of switches. For most of the switches, when I finally got there, I felt I'd made a mistake.

Hartman: It wasn't any better?

Sally: The switch wasn't the right thing. I had a problem with the loyalty, the having to stay whether you like it or not. No place is perfect. I suppose that's the message you should get across. If people are going to switch jobs they should be prepared for the fact that the next place won't be any better so they should at least get more money if they do it.

Keep in mind that everyone else is jumping too, so if you stick around you may end up moving up. A lot of people have executed it that way. I know some people who have stuck around and they haven't gone ahead and I've also known people who've stuck around and have done very well. So, you really need to make that assessment.

When I was with one bank, I got a 38 percent bonus and then I left about two months before I was about to be paid it again. That was tough. At this point, I wonder, if I'd stayed would I be as well off or possibly better off than I am now? But I would have been very unhappy and wouldn't have grown in terms of my skills, intellectually and professionally. Financially, it would have been great. It was an easy job and it would have been easy to stay there.

Wrapping It Up

Here you have a prototypical techno-jumper. Don't you love how she comes to the conclusion that full-time work with one company is just not for her? She can afford to have that attitude. This is one executive who has built such competitive skills that the demand for them is incredible. It's more profitable for her to do assignments with lots of different firms at whatever rate she chooses. All these benefits are bundled within working for a big six management consulting firm. Of course she sees this as a temporary situation until she can branch out on her own. This executive is taking a fast route to financial success, one that is not dependent on a job from one firm.

TEMPORARY STAFFING

■ Michael J. McGowan
   Senior Vice President and General Manager
   Major Temporary Staffing Company

Education
Michigan State University, BSEE in Digital Electronics and Communications, 1975. Michigan State University, MBA in Finance and Marketing, 1977.

Personal
Married with three children. Enjoys golfing, skiing, and spending time with his family. Also active in several civic and charitable organizations.

Hartman: You started your career at Automatic Data Processing (ADP) in 1977 and stayed until 1992. You had an incredible number of positions at ADP. Could you describe how you advanced?

McGowan: In 1977, I started in sales within the network services division, grew to sales manager, and in 1981, district manager, managing the entire Detroit automotive related business.

221

This position had both the sales and technical activities reporting up through me.

Later in 1984 I became director of strategic planning for the dealer services division, reporting directly to the president of the division. This role really provided me with a variety of experiences and the opportunity to learn a whole new business. Reporting to the president helped me gain more credibility and visibility within the company.

In 1985, I was promoted to vice president of strategic planning and business development, where I took on the additional responsibilities of joint venture, product, and company acquisitions for the division. One year later I took over responsibility for all communication-based products and services as the vice president and general manager with full P & L responsibility. Based upon our success, a new division was formed, the automotive information services division, and I assumed responsibility of vice president of marketing services in 1987. In 1988, the decision was made to consolidate these new offerings into existing business units, at which time I moved to the employer services division of ADP in Chicago as vice president of client relations. In 1991, I assumed the role of acting general manager of the Chicago region when my immediate manager (the Midwest division president) left the company.

Hartman: How did you change positions every one to two years at ADP?

McGowan: Most of them were mutual with respect to my career objectives and the goals and direction of the company. They all prepared me for more responsibility and further career progression. In a two-year stint you should be able to learn the business and the job, and make a contribution. The key in all these positions and career progressions is making contributions. Had I not made a contribution in a particular job, they would have moved me aside or moved me out!

Hartman: Could you describe the last job you had after fifteen years with ADP?

McGowan: My immediate manager had left the company and I became the acting general manager of the Chicago region. I had full P&L responsibility for this $60 million business, which included about 14,000 clients and 750 employees providing human resource and payroll services.

Hartman: Why did you go to The MEDSTAT Group?

McGowan: The MEDSTAT opportunity came about from a recruiter's call. He said, "We're looking for somebody that has client service, sales, strategic planning, national account selling, general management, marketing, and health-care experience." I said, "I've got all those except health-care, so why don't we keep on talking?" It was a tough decision to leave ADP. I knew everybody in the company up through the chairman and CEO. I had a great reputation there and exposure throughout the company as I had spent time in every major division except one.

The MEDSTAT position gave me the opportunity to actually run my own business as well as move to the exciting and dynamic health-care industry. At ADP, I was running a region— just a smaller piece of the larger pie. The second reason is that it moved us back to Detroit, which was home for both my wife and me.

Hartman: You started as regional vice president of the client services organization and then were promoted to vice president and general manager. Why did you leave after three years?

McGowan: I was recruited by a senior management consultant to the president and CEO of my current firm. The management consultant stated that they were looking for external talent to bring into senior management roles as they had been losing market share for a number of years and needed to change direction and focus. He felt that my background at ADP, my experience at MEDSTAT as a general manager, and my overall track record of positive business results and success would be a good match.

It also gave me the opportunity to manage an organization with $800 million in annualized revenue, a step up from my experience at ADP and MEDSTAT. Therefore, it was the next leap in pursuit of my overall career objectives.

Hartman: Have you ever marketed yourself to recruiters?

McGowan: I have always worked with recruiters and headhunters from a hiring perspective. Therefore, these same individuals have also been my personal network from a job search standpoint.

Hartman: Is there any advice you would like to provide to people who are considering a job change?

McGowan: One thing I've learned, especially being employed by a staffing firm, is that in effect we're all "temporary employees." We really are. Whether we're working for ourselves or a big company—we're a temporary employee. I think it's best for everybody once they realize that. It forces you to look inward and ask, "What am I producing for this particular company? What added value am I bringing? Why are they paying me *x* thousands of dollars and what do they get out of me?" It really forces you to think along the lines of "I can't count on this company to pay me for thirty years because I may be gone tomorrow. I need to make sure that I'm marketable. I must acquire skills through the years that will enable me to go somewhere else and earn a living." The days of real job security are over for most firms and employees. I think that's one of the most important things—we all are temporary employees. The sooner you realize it, the better.

The second point I would suggest is the necessity to always network, network, and network. That includes networking with those in recruiting roles I mentioned earlier as well as, and more importantly, friends and other personal and business associates. The majority of new positions are unadvertised and are filled through personal contacts.

Wrapping It Up

Michael McGowan espouses a very realistic and contemporary view of jobs today—"We are all temporary employees." Look at how he gained this perspective. Every one to two years for fifteen years he was promoted to a new job within his first company. Although he rose to acting general manager of the Chicago region, he recognized that an external offer would provide more opportunity and career progression. He jumped externally and then foresaw after three years that another external jump would provide yet another senior management position with even greater organizational, revenue, and business responsibility. This jump was also very timely because his employer, The MEDSTAT Group, was being acquired by a larger conglomerate.

This executive not only has the skills to do the job, but knows how and when to take them to the next job.

EPILOGUE

Let's return to the concept of You, Inc. If you're going to apply the latest management theories to You, Inc., you need to address Hamel and Prahalad's concept of transforming the future of industry: What's your industry? How are you going to transform your future?

If you're going to define the top, start with yourself. You can also learn from the careers of the executives in Part 3 of this book. See how they transformed their skill sets to make the next jump up. As for me, I think of the top as a series of infinite possibilities. It's doing what you want to do with the people you want to do it with. It's a moving target that has to have intellectual intrigue, be totally fun, and pay well.

Are you wondering whatever happened to that violinist thrown into the business world? After switching to business, I jumped every one to three years, working for Citibank and eight other companies. It took me over fourteen years to finally reach vice president, chief marketing officer, within a global corporation. Jumping was what got me there and I'd be there still if I hadn't written this book.

I decided to write "the perfect book proposal," as defined in Jeff Herman's book (*Write the Perfect Book Proposal*, John Wiley, 1993). Because I'm also a fan of database marketing, I used it to get published. Although I didn't know any literary agents or publishers, I figured that some of the people I knew might. I interrogated my database and chose the top 100 people who could best help me get this book published. I sent them my perfect book proposal a week before starting that new chief marketing officer job.

About five months later, I had a most memorable experience at work. I was spending the day immersed in the selection of mailing lists. I had over seventy list cards spread out in piles in my office and was trying to determine which lists we would use. My boss called me in to his office.

There was the human resources director, white-faced, hugging a manila file to his chest. He said to me, "Is this yours?" and showed me my book proposal. (God knows how *he* got it!) I said, "Of course that's mine and I'm proud of it! I had mentioned to [my boss] that I was trying to get a book published." The human resources man said, "You didn't say what the book was about!" I said, "You guys didn't ask, you didn't seem to be interested. It doesn't have anything to do with marketing anyway. OK, so it's an unpublished book proposal. What does this matter?" He said, "We've decided to terminate your employment. We find the content and material alarming. . . ." They went on to explain that they felt the material challenged the traditional value of loyalty to the firm (without mentioning that, yes, they had recruited me from another firm).

Needless to say, I was surprised. You never can assume that doing your job is your job. So there I was, out of a job I had just started. A week later I got my first of three offers on this book. So I finished the book and recruited. I can tell you it's definitely a rap looking for a job after being fired for writing a job-jumping book! I told everyone the truth and people alternated between horror and laughter.

I was on the West Coast for an interview and decided that I couldn't leave without doing some snowboarding. It was the perfect way to do some dreaming. The hot-tub scene at Squaw Valley resort on the slopes of Lake Tahoe is a superb playground. You descend down the hillside into night punctuated by thick, hot steam rising from outdoor floor-lit Jacuzzis. You slip in and relive the day's thrills and the night's birth. You lay your head back, recharge your body, and gaze at jeweled night skiing slopes under the stars. It's a place where you breathe your dreams.

I decided to go back to contracting and started with a contract opportunity as director of database marketing with an international advertising agency. I've never been on the agency side before. I'm learning quite a bit about interactive advertising and am using my database marketing skills. All the things that used to depreciate my ongoing compensation—benefits, signing, and exit bonuses—now increase the contract. By definition, contract work has a simpler, all-in-fee structure. Plus, between visits to offices and clients on the West Coast and in British Columbia, the magic of Whistler Mountain and Lake Tahoe make for very enticing weekends! Living begins with experiencing two feet of fresh snow at eight in the morning at the top of Whistler Mountain. For a snowboarder living in Chicago, this is true seduction.

Admittedly, when you consider the spectrum of jumping styles, I'm part of a smaller group that enjoys the risky side. I haven't changed much from my start as a musician, where you take your talents to a number of different groups. After switching to business, I jumped fast, gained marketable skills and credentials, became an author and a consultant. I've never had more fun and never enjoyed greater financial success than now.

My style has been to jump quickly across firms and professions, and this works for me. But there are many styles to jumping and only you can create yours.

INDEX

A Contest:
Calling All Employment
Negotiation Dialogues

What should you say to get a signing bonus or to increase your severance pay? Check out Chapter Seven, "Get Paid Coming and Going," for five bonus dialogues that earned me a total of $82,000. Chapter Eight includes three more dialogues that were used for negotiating new job offers.

But let's face it—the only way we are really going to learn the best strategies is to share our collective experiences. I'm sponsoring an ongoing contest for the best employment-negotiation dialogues. I will post some of these stories on the Internet and offer a free *Strategic Job Jumping* book to each of the top twenty dialogues. E-mail your dialogues to:

jh@juliahartman.com

Go ahead and enjoy telling us your story! How did you negotiate a windfall? What did you say to get a bonus and what did your boss say? How did you structure the compensation for a job you love?

If you win, you will be contacted. If you want anonymity, you've got it. Of course, it's understood that your dialogue could end up on the Internet or in my next book!

A Journey into the Heroic Environment

A Personal Guide to Creating a Work Environment
Built on Shared Values

Rob Lebow

ISBN 0-7615-0904-6 / paperback / 224 pages
U.S. $13.00 / Can. $17.95

"I loved this simple, powerful book. Buy it!"
—Harvey Mackay, author of *Swim with the Sharks Without Being Eaten Alive*

Two strangers' chance encounter leads us all on a compelling journey into the fascinating and stimulating new Shared Values work environment, where all workers and their ideas are treated with dignity and respect. This modern business classic has been newly revised and updated to reflect 25 years of research—including 17 million surveys from 40 countries—into what people really want in their workplace. A quiz allows you to evaluate your work environment's capacity for Shared Values.

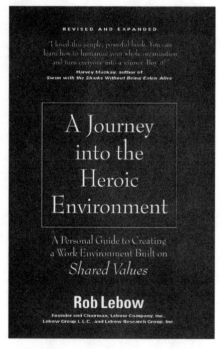

Visit us online at http://www.primapublishing.com

Cubicle Warfare

*Self-Defense Strategies for Today's
Hyper-Competitive Workplace*

Blaine Pardoe

ISBN 0-7615-1066-4 / paperback / 240 pages
U.S. $16.00 / Can. $21.95

This take-no-prisoners guide reveals the rules of warfare in the modern workplace—and how you can play to win. Written by a veteran corporate training manager, it explains how to draft and execute a battle plan for professional success. Tactics include mastering short- and long-term career goals, distinguishing friends from foes, brown-nosing for fun and profit, and much more. There's even a field guide to the seven personality types found in the typical office, a quiz to determine where you fit in, and a survival manual for people who prefer to stay out of the office war games.

Do you *Still* Think
Office Politics Don't Matter

Visit us online at http://www.primapublishing.com

To Order Books

Please send me the following items:

Quantity	Title	Unit Price	Total
_____	Cubicle Warfare	$ 16.00	$ _____
_____	A Journey Into the Heroic Environment	$ 13.00	$ _____
_____	_____	$ _____	$ _____
_____	_____	$ _____	$ _____
_____	_____	$ _____	$ _____

*Shipping and Handling depend on Subtotal.			
Subtotal	**Shipping/Handling**		
$0.00–$14.99	$3.00		
$15.00–$29.99	$4.00		
$30.00–$49.99	$6.00		
$50.00–$99.99	$10.00		
$100.00–$199.99	$13.50		
$200.00+	Call for Quote		

Foreign and all Priority Request orders:
Call Order Entry department
for price quote at 916-632-4400

This chart represents the total retail price of books only (before applicable discounts are taken).

Subtotal $ _____

Deduct 10% when ordering 3-5 books $ _____

7.25% Sales Tax (CA only) $ _____

8.25% Sales Tax (TN only) $ _____

5.0% Sales Tax (MD and IN only) $ _____

7.0% G.S.T. Tax (Canada only) $ _____

Shipping and Handling* $ _____

Total Order $ _____

By Telephone: With MC or Visa, call 800-632-8676 or 916-632-4400.
Mon–Fri, 8:30-4:30.

WWW: http://www.primapublishing.com

By Internet E-mail: sales@primapub.com

By Mail: Just fill out the information below and send with your remittance to:

**Prima Publishing
P.O. Box 1260BK
Rocklin, CA 95677**

My name is _____

I live at _____

City _____ State _____ ZIP _____

MC/Visa# _____ Exp. _____

Check/money order enclosed for $ _____ Payable to Prima Publishing

Daytime telephone _____

Signature _____